"In a conversation some years ago, Esther Meek suggested to me that our first knowledge as human beings is the knowledge of being loved—in the wombs, at the breast, and in the embraces of our mothers. This first knowledge, she suggested, is paradigmatic for all of our knowing. To know follows being known; being known is woven into being loved. This suggestion has, ever since, been shaping my epistemology as a scholar, but more deeply, my understanding of my knowing as a human being in all of life. Readers of this *A Little Manual for Knowing* are embarking on an adventure that may, similarly, make a decisive difference in their learning and in all of their lives."

—GIDEON STRAUSS
Executive Director, Max De Pree Center for Leadership,
Fuller Theological Seminary

"With this pearl of great value, Esther Meek lovingly and confidently shepherds us on a pilgrimage, a reconsidering and recovery of what it means to know. Her *A Little Manual* not only is about epistemology; indwelling it—reading the text and reflecting on its exercises—is to practice and experience epistemology. For those who commit to the journey, the hoped for gifts await."

—BRUCE A. VOJAK
Associate Dean of Engineering, University of Illinois at Urbana-Champaign

"When I read anything Esther Meek writes I find myself with holy envy longing to be a wiser man. This brilliant little manual captures the depth and simplicity of her work and invites the reader to apply wisdom to real life complexities and problems. Esther's wisdom is immense, playful, and heart transforming. This manual will inform, enlighten, and free you to know how to know in new ways that will transform your heart."

—DAN B. ALLENDER
Professor of Counseling Psychology and Founding President, The Seattle School of Theology and Psychology

"If I were asked to choose one key curriculum to be taught in a freshman class of any liberal arts university, it would be Esther Meeks's class on epistemology. If I were asked to choose one book, it would be *A Little Manual for Knowing*. At (the) Fujimura home we choose one book each summer to read together and discuss with our grown children. This year it will be *A Little Manual for Knowing*—essential reading for every university, every business, every church, and every home."

—MAKOTO FUJIMURA
artist

A LITTLE MANUAL
FOR KNOWING

A Little Manual for
KNOWING

Esther Lightcap Meek

 CASCADE *Books* • Eugene, Oregon

A LITTLE MANUAL FOR KNOWING

Cascade Books
An Imprint of Wipf and Stock Publishers
199 W. 8th Ave., Suite 3
Eugene, OR 97401

www.wipfandstock.com

ISBN 13: 978-1-61097-784-5

Cataloguing-in-Publication data:

Meek, Esther Lightcap.

A little manual for knowing / Esther Lightcap Meek.

xvii + 104 pp. ; 23 cm. Includes bibliographical references.

ISBN 13: 978-1-61097-784-5

1. Knowledge, Theory of (Religion). 2. Christianity—Philosophy. I. Title.

BT50 M44 2014

Manufactured in the U.S.A.

For my family:
Starr and Alex, Stacey and Evan, Steph and Garrett,
and the budding generation

And for Dr. Robert M. Frazier,
colleague and friend

With wonder and gratitude

Contents

Introduction

THIS IS A LITTLE book about knowing. It is meant especially for a person, or team of persons, starting out on a knowing venture. That venture could be college. It could be starting or joining a business. It could be creating art, doing scientific research, or designing a bridge. It could be cooking or playing sports. It could be starting a relationship with a person or with a place. It could be self-discovery. It could be a relationship with God, or ministry in a church team. These are everyday adventures. They can be once-in-a-lifetime quests. This *Little Manual* will help all such ventures.

Epistemology: concrete ideas about knowledge and knowing

We're involved in knowing all the time in all corners of our lives. Even so, we tend not to think about knowing *itself*. We don't—unless a puzzle arises. Beginning a venture is just such a puzzle. How do we come to know? Whose guidance do we trust? How do we know we are getting it right about the situation? About ourselves? How, after all, does knowing work? Apart from some savvy about these things, the success of our venture is in jeopardy. This *Little Manual* is about how knowing works.

How we know is actually a philosophical question. It is what epistemology, one of the major areas of philosophy, is all about. Philosophy concerns the profoundest wonders of our lives as humans. It concerns life's shaping questions: What is really real? (metaphysics or ontology). How do I know it? (epistemology).

1

What is right and good? (metaethics and axiology). What does it mean to be human? (philosophical anthropology). Our entire lives sail on the breast of these deep, wonder-full questions. They are not the sort of questions we can solve by doing a science experiment. We slowly gain insight into them as we live our lives and continually reflect on our living. Philosophy accompanies the trajectory of our growing to understand what it means to be human, a trajectory from wonder to wisdom that never leaves the wonder behind.

Our common, tacit, epistemic orientation

Many people don't think much about how we know because we take it for granted. But we tacitly presume some things about knowing. We tend to think knowledge is information, facts, bits of data, "content," true statements—true statements justified by other true statements. And while this isn't exactly false, we tend to have a vision of knowledge as being *only* this. We conclude that gaining knowledge is collecting information—and we're done—educated, trained, expert, certain.

This is a philosophical orientation, an unexamined one. It has a lot of appeal, because it is quantifiable, measurable, assessable, and commodifiable. It offers control and power. But we'll see that the knowledge-as-information vision is actually defective and damaging. It distorts reality and humanness, and it gets in the way of good knowing.

If knowledge is information, and either we have it or we don't, how can we come to know in the first place? What does discovery involve? Or learning? Or insight? Or the creative act? How do we get going on a knowing venture?

Along with this knowledge-as-information approach, we tend to be "epistemological dualists." We distinguish knowledge from belief, facts from values, reason from faith, theory from application, thought from emotion, mind from body, objective from subjective, science from art. We readily overlay the first members of each pair—knowledge, facts, reason, theory, mind, objectivity, and science. And we set each first member over against its "opposite." We think we need to keep knowledge "pure" from these "opposites."

For example, we believe that we should keep ourselves and our passion out of knowledge if we are to be objective. So we actually cut off knowledge from ourselves, the knowers. As a result, we can be bored or indifferent about knowledge.

Here's another example: we think that knowledge is information or theory, and that application and action is something else—and thus, not knowledge. We can think that knowledge actually has little to do with real life. Maybe knowledge doesn't matter anyway.

We know there is something called wisdom. But how wisdom connects with knowledge—what wisdom even is, and how it may be had—we have no idea.

Epistemological dualism cuts us as knowers down into disconnected compartments unable to work together—information here, body there, emotions in a third place. It depersonalizes us at the moment of one of our greatest opportunities for personhood—coming to know. It dispels any sense of adventure.

Another sort of distinction we can find ourselves making is between knowledge and reality—the known. We may think that we can be sure of data, but we cannot be sure of what is really the case. Knowledge is just convenient summaries of data.

And then we can move on to think that "knowledge" is just what we take it to be, because knowing—understanding the world—isn't even possible. We can even think that what we call "knowledge" is really about power and convention and what works. We can think that truth is ours to determine.

Disconnecting knowing from knower and known is not a helpful mindset for starting a knowing venture. It dismissively suspects the thing we want to come to know. It doesn't give us confidence or savvy about the venture. It offers zero strategy for moving from zero to sixty in coming to understand anything at all.

Reorienting our epistemic stance

These last paragraphs are packed with mystifying thoughts and questions. But they make a few things clear. First, people do have plenty of ideas about knowledge and knowing. Second, those ideas are, by definition, epistemology. We are philosophical beings whether or not we have had a class in philosophy. In fact, we live out an orientation to knowing. Third, these ideas about knowledge can be expected to affect our knowing. Fourth, thinking of knowledge as information is an epistemic stance that does not help make sense of knowing ventures. We may need epistemological therapy.

We are epistemological beings: we live out an orientation to knowing, whether we "know" it or not. And that orientation probably needs some therapy. This *Little Manual* will help you reorient your tacitly presumed epistemology to something more effective and human.

People tend to think that philosophy is abstract and impractical. That's because it takes effort to probe these things. There aren't pat answers. It takes personal risk. But in fact, philosophy is concrete and powerfully practical. If you don't fix it, it will put you and your world and your venture in a fix. If you do fix it, it will open the world to you. It will make you far better at your venture and at your life. That is the promise of this *Little Manual.*

Proposing covenant epistemology

In my own journey of puzzlement and inquiry and philosophy, I have developed an approach to knowing that I call *covenant epistemology.* My own urgent life questions have always been epistemic. The single most helpful insight I uncovered in my personal search was Michael Polanyi's epistemology of "subsidiary-focal integration." Ever since I found it, it has made concretely practical sense of all my knowings in all dimensions of my life. I found that it opens all kinds of vistas and turns coming to know into delightful adventure. It makes you better at knowing. I and many others have found it to be personally healing. The *Little Manual* will get you on board with "SFI" in chapter 4.

I was twenty-four or so when I first encountered SFI. I have lived out this approach for decades now. Over the years I found that it signposted and invited a larger vision of knowing, as well as of reality and life. I have come to believe we should think of knower and known as persons in relationship, where knowing is the relationship. This relationship has covenantal dimensions. By that I mean that the knower pledges her- or himself to the yet-to-be-known, the way a groom pledges himself to a bride. SFI plus the covenantal interpersonhood of knower and known is what I have in mind by covenant epistemology. Covenant epistemology both reorients our knowing therapeutically and offers a life-shaping vision.

About the *Little Manual*

I have already written two books on the subject of knowing. *Longing to Know* (2003) developed SFI to address in a fresh way the question whether we can know God. Readers easily saw it also held concrete applications to business, to art, to counseling, to education, to engineering, to athletics, even to detective work. I took the next eight years to put into words the further development of covenant epistemology, along with a philosophical argument in its defense: *Loving to Know* appeared in 2011. Readers of this book regularly undergo personal transformation.

This *Little Manual* is a short introductory manual useful for a quick but therapeutic entrée in connection with a wide variety of knowing ventures. The *Little Manual* can leave a lot out because the earlier books have gone over the ground carefully. Specifically, it leaves out citations. You can find, at the back of this book, a list of the sources of the key ideas that covenant epistemology adapts from others' work. All references here are documented in the other books. It also leaves out extensive argumentation. But if the *Little Manual* tantalizes you in further study, consider reading the others.

The exercises are important!

Each little chapter of this book offers a copious amount of exercises for your own knowing venture. In a key way, these exercises are the most important part of the book. A manual is a how-to; that means you have to engage in the how-to. No ordinary person enjoys reading directions for the fun of it. Nor do we generally understand the directions and diagrams unless we are actually trying to do what they say. Similarly, with just about every sentence in this book, you'll find it makes sense in light of your own firsthand experience of your knowing venture. The exercises are there to prompt such important engagement. "Manual," after all, has something to do etymologically with *hand*.

Also, personalize the text and the exercises at every point possible to your own discipline or area of inquiry. College students should read it as about the college experience; business persons as about business; artists as about the creative act, would-be seekers of relationship—with others or with God—as just that. That you can do this will underscore a key emphasis of the *Little Manual*: knowing works like this in any field.

For everybody, not just Christians

My life and work have been shaped in the Christian tradition. It stands to reason that if you believe in the God of the Judeo-Christian Scriptures, you would think it important to develop an epistemology that accommodates knowing God. Dealing God into knowing, of course, means dealing him into the epistemic driver's seat. Knowing him would be formative for knowing anything. At the same time, Scripture indicates that God actually accords hospitable space to his creation and to creaturely knowers. Real freedom is had because it is conferred generously by a personal Other.

What's more, in this view, we ourselves are not God; we are *creaturely* knowers. Our glory as humans is to know from a particular place and orientation, to journey toward what we do not yet know. Always we are on the way. We are on the way with respect to knowing God as well as knowing our world. We understand partially. We know as we give ourselves and as we are known. And Christian believers are not thereby more assured of "A"s on exams, nor of a successful business venture.

So this is a manual for *all* knowing ventures for *all* persons, no matter their religious orientation. For all that, if you are looking for it, covenant epistemology signposts knowing this God, and can lead you to him. Every act of insight suggests his giving, his coming, his redemptive knowing of us. And knowing him actually can make you better at knowing anything.

Epiphany: pilgrimage and gift

The well-known biblical story of the Magi who journey to find the Christ child and to bring gifts offers an emblematic story of knowing. They are not called wise men for nothing! Nor is it a meaningless accident that we use the word *epiphany* in referring to a moment of insight. Epiphany is the name of the church season in which we celebrate God's revealing himself to these Gentiles—and to us.

Consider the Magi. Arabian astrologers, for years they had bound themselves to study what they half-understood. They studied the planets and stars, not for mere facts and figures about the planets, but because they pursued deeper meaning. They were not "collecting data," building a bank of comprehensive information. They attended to the stars, we may surmise, in a loving and wondering search for wisdom: wisdom of the sort that comes to expression in a harrowing pilgrimage together beyond Arabia, across trackless wastes, across tense racial and political boundaries, into the unknown to find a foreign king to whom they deemed a certain star to belong, a king worth worshipping with their best gifts—treasures themselves fraught with portent. They bound themselves covenantally to the yet-to-be-known, in their growing expertise, to invite its gracious disclosure of deeper meaning. They bound themselves to that as-yet-unknown reality in taking up such a journey. What they actually found surprisingly transformed their half-understood inquiries as reality swept in and swept them up.

Knowing is a *pilgrimage*. It requires taking personal responsibility, born of love, to pledge allegiance to what we do not yet know. It requires relying on seemingly opaque guidance to venture into the darkness of half-understanding. We invite its gracious and surprising self-disclosure, seeking to indwell its clues to make sense of a hidden pattern. We risk our forever being changed. It is an adventure.

Knowing is a pilgrimage *together*. The *Little Manual* addresses persons joining a team of explorers who intend to venture together toward knowing. But even if your journey seems a solitary one, at any point in it you can recognize how others have contributed to your journey, and how you can avail yourself of the camaraderie of others as you go forward. Reality proves to be richly multi-faceted. Working with others in our knowing venture, we can pool our diverse perspectives and training so that we can engage the world even more responsibly and effectively.

Knowing is a *gift*. Epiphany comes as a surprising encounter, equal parts knowing and being known. It could never have been achieved in a systematic or linear fashion. It transforms knower and known. Deep insight hints of exciting future prospects, confirming that we have made contact with reality. Pilgrimage modulates into an ongoing dance of communion. Reality proves to be deeply dynamic and welcomes us in. Knowing ushers in shalom.

Your knowing venture

You may be starting college. College is a knowing venture if anything is! Incoming freshmen, or any student poised on the brink of a fresh semester, will do well to give thought to whether learning involves more than amassing information, and how profound insight may be had. Any business venture involves coming to understand—a market, a product, a company, the past, the future. Business, like college, unavoidably binds knowledge to investment. Human endeavors such as scientific research, technological design, artistic creation, athletics, and human services, all involve knowing ventures. Effective practice in each involves the features and strategies this *Little Manual* identifies. Fulfilling a mission as a team is a knowing venture. Any sort of quest for self-discovery or growing interpersonal relationship is a knowing venture.

On the brink of what knowing venture do you stand? This little book offers pilgrim knowers a manual for the journey. I believe it also offers the prospect of joy.

Exercises for your knowing venture

From the following list, choose a few questions that you find especially suited to your knowing venture at this time. If you are part of a team, discuss your responses to these questions with the team, and as a team. Designating some time for this conversation should be part of your strategy in your knowing venture. Follow these directions for the questions at the end of every chapter.

1. Brainstorm, and list as many different sorts of knowing ventures you can think of.

2. What would you say is your current knowing venture?

3. What would you say is the thing you want to know, or the achievement you desire?

4. Tell the story of the origin of this venture. How does the story already display features of a journey or pilgrimage together?

5. Here at the outset of your venture, what puzzles do you have about knowing? Are there other times in your life where you have or have had similar puzzles?

6. Think of any examples that display an underlying knowledge-as-information orientation. Identify any ways you see that this approach might limit knowing ventures.

7. How does it help you and your knowing venture to see humans as philosophical? How does it make it harder?

8. Rate, on a scale from 1 to 10, the level of your commitment for this venture. Explain why you picked the number you did.

9. What skills must you acquire as part of this venture? What will it take to acquire them?

10. Do you have a team in this venture? Briefly describe them and what they bring to the venture.

11. What other resources do you have to draw on?

12. How might this book be a resource for your knowing venture?

PART I

Pilgrimage

CHAPTER 1

Love

C HANCES ARE YOU THINK it strange to be setting out on a venture of knowing by talking about love. How can you love what you do not know? Do we not first know and then, possibly, love? Knowledge has nothing to do with love, anyway. Love would get in the way of facts. Love is an emotion. It's subjective and not rational. Love may be "all you need," but the songwriter didn't have in mind starting a business or going to college. Love isn't going to crack the code of reality. We need information.

This kind of thinking reveals an underlying epistemic orientation of knowledge-as-information. Our unexamined preconceptions of what knowledge is tend to disconnect talk of love and relationship from knowledge. This outlook, this *Little Manual* proposes, can hamper any knowing venture. Epistemological therapy is needed.

This little manual offers such therapy. But right here at the beginning, the reader will have to decide to trust the *Little Manual* that this will happen. This can be offensive and threatening. But it too is an epistemic matter. Exercising some kind of trust at the beginning of a knowing venture, and even throughout it, proves to be a necessary and helpful epistemic practice.

Knowing and being go hand in hand

To begin talking about love in knowing, first we need to say something about reality and life. Epistemology and metaphysics can't help but go hand in hand. Reality is what we know. What we think of the one shapes what we think of the other. If you find that you think there is nothing more to reality than what lab experiments uncover or our eyes see, a little additional thought should show that this claim itself is not the sort of thing that lab experiments could ever uncover or eyes ever see. It is a metaphysical and epistemological claim. And it is the sort of claim that shapes what we think we see and how we understand knowing ventures. Metaphysics is unavoidable. It is deeply concrete and practical.

This book tackles things from the knowing side of the connected pair. But we can expect that the orientation the *Little Manual* helps you develop will in turn reshape your generally tacit view of reality. And here at the beginning, we have to say something about reality to start to make sense of why knowing begins with love.

Reality: impersonal bits or personal gift?

Our knowledge-as-information orientation additionally shapes our picture of reality. It tends to reduce reality to two-dimensional ones and zeros, impersonal bits, so much data to be collected. This way of seeing the world fits with our epistemic view that gaining knowledge means passively collecting impersonal information. The goal in this approach to knowledge can be to eliminate any mystery from an indifferent universe, amassing all the bits, eventually gaining comprehensive knowledge. It is a kind of mastery or conquest.

On the contrary, the *Little Manual* will say, reality is *gift*, and love is at the core of all things. It is not impersonal; rather, reality is person-like. It is not passive and inert. It is richly multi-faceted, deeply dynamic, ever new and surprising, never to be sapped of mystery. We must reorient our epistemic relationship to it to be more like a dance of overture and response, of wooing and being wooed. We must replace indifferent distance with intimate care.

You may be familiar with an episode of the original *Star Trek* TV series, called "The Devil in the Dark." Captain James T. Kirk and *Enterprise* crew at first take the Horta to be a massive boulder. The Horta, they discover with surprise, is a being—a mother protecting her eggs. Figuring that out changes the way they relate to the Horta from impersonal to interpersonal, and they make real progress in knowing reality. They gain understanding, and peace is restored. Changing your view from seeing reality as impersonal to seeing it as personal would be a shift such as this.

The idea of reality as gift seems to be a theological vision—the sort of thing we associate with religion. But it's easily arguable that humans are incurably religious. People are even religious in their irreligion. However, religion or the justification of a theological vision is not the point of this book. Reality as gift is a metaphysical view that goes with the restored orientation in knowing that this *Little Manual* aids.

In fact, even apart from religion it can be seen that people tend to personify things. Where we have presumed that reality is impersonal, of course this seems an unwarranted superimposition. But why should we think that reality is, first, impersonal? Perhaps our latent metaphysic has depersonalized what is fundamentally personal.

Reality's normative features

How can it be that reality is gift? No matter what thing in the world you think about, whether a spider plant or a biome, a clothes pin or a computer, that thing is made up of "stuff," but it also has a certain "what-it-is-to-be-this-thing." We can name the characteristics that make it what it is. The thing holds promise to continue to be what it is. We also use these characteristics to judge the excellence or inferiority of the particular specimen we are looking at—a "way-it-ought-to-be."

If you think about this, these features are normative. This means that there is an oughtness about them. Mere stuff cannot account for oughtness. But oughtness has to be there for there to be stuff. When you think about why things are the way they are, why they are there instead of not there, and how they came to be in the first place, whatever else is true about these questions, this normative dimension is necessary. Nature is not enough, as one writer puts it. He goes on to argue that reality is gift.

These normative elements are covenantal-promise or pledge-like. They involve words that don't describe, so much as enact or decree reality. Covenant makes reality.

It is intriguing that, in the Christian Scripture's story of creation, God says, "Let there be . . ." and then there is. (This has nothing to do with the question of evolution; oughtness makes reality, however it comes about.) I can relate to this easily when I think of all the birthday party games I invented over my children's young lives, and all the classes I have invented over my students' lives. I have said plenty of "let there be's," which have brought realities to be. Also, when my daughters each said "I do" at their weddings, they said something normative; they generously let something be, and that brought reality to be.

Normative . . . covenantal . . . interpersonal . . . gift . . . love is at the core of all things

And such words of pledge and promise suggest a relationship of persons in which they are embedded. Normative elements require a larger context of persons in relation as persons. If all real things require a "let there be," a normative dimension, they require a larger context of persons in which promise and covenant and gift pertain.

Covenant and promise are highly sophisticated interpersonal pronouncements. They are free; they might not have been pronounced. So they are gifts. They are persons' acts of love. They are commitments of love.

Gift has a normativity about it. A gift involves a ceremonial presentation, and appropriate manners. Gift-giving is something that only persons can enact. Like laughter, gift-giving and person-hood always occur together—you can have neither without the presence of the other. Gift giving involves consent, a highly sophisticated, generous, letting be. Another thing that the idea of gift suggests is self-giving, and readiness on the part of reality to lavish us excessively. This is how love is at the core of all things.

Normativity, we may think, need not be gift. It could be, simply, law. We all can see that reality is law-like. But law itself is the enactment of persons—persons who need not have said let there be. That something might not be but yet is is occasion for wonder and gratitude—assuming that the might-not-be is good. In fact, in reality we do see law, and we do find much that prompts wonder, including law that prompts wonder. Law itself is gift.

So to think of reality as gift showcases the normative elements in reality. The normative dimension suggests the interpersonal context. It implies that reality is gift.

Thinking of reality as gift helps realign our orientation in knowing it. For how you respond to a gift is highly personal. It must be so, for the gift enactment to be genuine. If love is at the core of all things, if reality is, at its core, the highly sophisticated interpersonal act of gift, then knowing is quite sensibly a responding gesture of love. *We love in order to know.* Love, not bare information amassing, should characterize the way we relate to the world. And like the Horta, the world repays this shift in orientation.

In the Christian theological vision, obviously God is the one covenanting, promising, gifting, reality into existence. He is covenantally binding himself to the ongoing charactered reality and nature of my spider plant. No matter how, mechanically speaking, it comes to be, he continues to word it into existence. Whether or not you think you believe in God, attending to these normative dimensions of reality, and to reality as interpersoned gift, will make you more effective at your knowing ventures.

Love vs. curse and obsession

How can we count on it being love at the core of all things? Life seems to contain as much curse as it does love. In fact, curses are "let there be"s that are not loving. Curse, too, is normative. It brings brokenness and hurt to be. Curse is connected with broken promises and betrayal. So curse implies a larger context of blessing and of pledge. Curse is devastating. But for this reason curse can never totally wipe out blessing. The good will win.

Also, what about obsession? Can you love something too much? Obsession is an unhealthy form of relating to something. It is selfish and possessive, driven by power. We should not call it love. Love accords space and true otherness to the other rather than seeking to absorb it. It involves a pledge to accord space and dignity to the other. Obsession is not an effective knowing practice. Obsession precludes knowing. But thinking about obsession, like thinking about curse, helps us see the kind of love that knowing should involve.

We need to ask ourselves whether we as knowers labor under threat, betrayal, or curse. If knowing involves self-giving love, these things hinder our readiness to know. There may prove to be other things that need to be addressed before we are free to attend to our knowing venture.

We also need to ask whether the desire we have to know is obsession rather than love. For reality not to be damaged and for our knowing to be true to reality, our love needs to be true and responsible self-giving.

Loving in order to know

But the most important thing we need to ask ourselves is whether we love in order to know. Do we bring to our knowing venture the love that will invite knowing? What does this look like? And how can we "up" our love?

What does it mean to love in order to know? And how does this approach aid our knowing ventures? The loving-to-know approach helps us notice and take seriously some things that in our heart of hearts we sense have everything to do with knowing—things that the knowledge-as-information approach doesn't accredit or allow, and therefore can't tap: things like desire, wonder, notice, and self-giving.

Knowing ventures begin out of love or desire. This starting point is the watershed difference between the knowledge-as-information approach and the loving-to-know approach to knowing. You do not just show up and indifferently start gathering information. Or if you do, you should not consider that a true knowing venture. It is desire that shapes the venture into a venture in the first place. To begin to know, we should uncover and tap into our desire. Knowing rides the wave of our desire.

Active and receptive; love, wonder, and notice

The dynamic of loving, or caring, in order to know, blends receptive and active sides. It is an active receptivity, or a receptive activity. It looks for the other to give, and it gives itself for the sake of the other. It is a kind of receptive waiting that humbly consents to the being of, and invites the coming of, the as yet hidden real. But this emptied waiting is a pledged self-giving. Love is the gift of the self. It takes a gift of the self in order to know. So it is active as well as receptive. This active receptivity is like exercising hospitality, welcoming someone into your space. Knowing, we can say, is hospitality. (Hospitality is a kind of responsive gift.) Every step of a knowing venture displays love's receptive and active sides. This active receptivity characterizes the entire pilgrimage of coming to know.

Active receptivity is right there at the beginning of any knowing venture. It is impossible to say which comes first, the active or the receptive. What starts the venture is notice and wonder. Something about reality catches our attention. To start to know is actually first a response to a dimly heard beckoning of the wonderfull real. If we can see knowing as a relationship between knower and known, we can see that reality makes the first overture. We can associate this call with our sense of wonder. Any geologist can probably name the day she or he first noticed and was taken in wonder by a rock. Every different discipline would involve something similar.

But wonder takes noticing. To notice and wonder at something is itself a highly sophisticated act that must occur for you to come to know. You actively attend to something significant. You assign value to it as something to notice, picking it out from a background. And you must *consent* to the wonder, give yourself to it, responding hospitably to its overture. This seemingly tiny first response is big with sophisticated interpersonhood. It is like saying "please": small but normative and momentous. It makes the wonder what it is.

But here is the thing: it takes love to notice and to wonder. A reality where love is the core of all things is one attuned to be seen only through eyes of love. Only when we first love do we begin to attend, to listen, to understand, to know. Why would we think that reality would disclose itself to uncaring, indifferent, suspicious, "knowers"?!

We can and should cultivate wonder—a posture of wonder. This is a trained readiness to be astounded. The readiness is that of a lover anticipating being delighted. Such training doesn't quell wonder; it enhances it. It broadens the range of our capacity to wonder.

Pledge and pilgrimage ahead

Once we are wondering and noticing, we may responsibly choose to give ourselves to a pilgrimage that reality seems to invite. We give ourselves to that inexplicable desire that is somehow the heart of our humanness. Our knowing venture taps into this desire. We open up to the wonder in love. We start to anticipate its gracious self-disclosure.

Our knowing venture is going to unfold in an ongoing dance of mutuality between knower and known, in active receptivity. It's something that we can learn to identify, trust ourselves to, and be intentional in tapping.

Knowing together with others

Caring in order to know is often best done—actually, inevitably done—*together* with others. Not even a solitary knower is ever entirely solitary. A solitary knower has already appropriated a language, a culture, a tradition. Each knower has submitted to authoritative guides in order to be taught or trained. Each has embraced a shared way of seeing the world. Each has acquired skill sets and formal theoretical frameworks.

But we all have a unique way of seeing and relating to the world, too. We are each utterly distinct persons. Out of our distinct love, we notice distinct aspects of reality, and reality responds to us along the lines of our distinctive care. Also, we all view life from a vantage point at least slightly different from anyone else's. And our experiences and training distinguish us from each other. Yet, as persons, we can share and delight in our differences.

We can capitalize on the diversity we bring to a team in our caring in order to know. But we only capitalize on knowing together when we covenant together in mutual trust. Groups of knowers who exhibit solidarity and conviviality invite the real more effectively. So in knowing we give ourselves in pledge to the yet-to-be-known, and we give ourselves in pledge to our team. Both will eventuate in a pilgrimage to knowing.

Friendship: the goal of knowing

Finally, this reorientation in knowing suggests something about the goal of knowing. The goal is no longer comprehensive, mystery-eliminating, reality-denuding information. The goal is communion—the communion of knower and known. Communion is the fulfillment of love. The goal is ongoing friendship. Friendship requires our ongoing pledge.

Rest and shalom in the adventure of knowing

This vision of knowing takes into its own generous view every corner of our lives and our world, every knowing venture. It makes us better persons and more effective knowers. It gives meaning to our lives and work. It governs the way we treat the world.

This orientation alone yields rest and shalom in our adventures in knowing. *Rest:* We may be at peace with our own efforts to know—with their long journey, their incompleteness and particularity, with their dependence on others and on the real itself. We may be confident in our distinct contributions, and confident in the risk. We may delight in the venture. We may hope for and joy in deepening communion with the real. *Shalom:* This approach honors, heals, and transformatively cultivates the real itself. Humans and societies may hope to be healers and friends of the world.

The love that launched your knowing venture

If you are embarking on a knowing venture, you no doubt have already loved, noticed, and wondered. It is good to identify these all-important gestures that you have already "committed." As you identify them, you can start to be intentional about them. You can be intentional about casting your knowing orientation and your knowing venture in light of them. This is the posture of loving in order to know.

If you are in a business, joining a business, or starting a business, there is something that you love that you are pursuing. In your care, you have noticed something remarkable about the world, something that suggests exciting future prospects. You have noticed something about people, or about society or culture, that you want to attend to and let draw you into a creative response. And you seek a creative response from reality.

It would be something very much the same for artists, designers, or innovators. It would be the same for caregivers or service providers. You want to identify the love, the notice, the wonder as you love in order to know.

If you are poised on the brink of a course of study you may have to determine whether in fact you do love in order to know. Maybe you find that you have come to it not because you love it—yet. You may be where you are because someone else loves it, or because you think you have to. All of us find ourselves in this situation at some time or other.

Perhaps you find yourself wonder-less: there isn't anything you care about in this situation. You may have fallen into a mismatch of your loves and your life. You may need to cast about in your life to identify things you do care about and do what you can to blow on the coals of your care. Doing this means risking giving up on one knowing venture to embrace another.

Or there may be a way to recast your venture so that it catches the current of your love. For all of us, entering a knowing venture requires at some point that we trust: We must trust others who know what we do not yet know, about the world, even about ourselves. We may need to trust another's love and notice and wonder. A responsible decision to trust is a centrally effective knowing practice, a posture of pledge-like love. Do not despise it, but rather embrace it with resolve.

We may need to trust ourselves to reality. But this is just the heart of coming to know what we do not yet know. All knowing is coming to know. So all knowing calls for giving ourselves to what we do not yet know. And this is loving in order to know. Of course it feels risky. Welcome to the pilgrimage that is a knowing venture.

You may find yourself in severe circumstances, sorely betrayed and numb, in danger and needy. Your knowing venture may be bare survival—and then healing. This is indeed horrific, and the horrific happens. We cannot make light of it or dismiss it.

But reality as dynamically, generously personal is capable of bringing healing, even in difficult circumstances. Indeed, hardship and affliction may mysteriously yield wisdom and authenticity, readiness for deeper wonder and knowing. This graced process is key to every knowing venture you undertake. Be patient, gentle with yourself, and thus invite the real.

Exercises for your knowing venture

1. Discuss some examples that show that reality is gift.

   a. How does it change people's outlook to see reality this way?

   b. How does this orientation impact your knowing venture?

2. In your chosen knowing venture, what has prompted your wonder?

   a. Tell the story of noticing the things that drew you to the venture.

   b. Identify the receptive and active sides of your wonder and noticing.

3. Or if there is nothing prompting your wonder in connection with the venture as it is, what are some other things that prompt your wonder? These may be entirely outside the venture, or there may be some other aspects of the venture that induce your wonder.

   a. Discuss the possibility that these other wonders might fuel a better, alternative venture.

   b. Discuss the difference this makes to your planned knowing venture.

4. How does it shape your outlook on your anticipated knowing venture to think of it as loving-in-order-to-know?

5. What concrete maxims and strategies does a "loving-in-order-to-know" approach suggest for your knowing venture?

CHAPTER 2

Pledge

YOU CAN SEE FROM the last chapter why this next one must be about pledge. Pledge, or covenant, is the "I do" of love. If we love in order to know, we pledge in order to love. We give ourselves, and we consent, in pledge. Additionally, pledge is key to inviting the real, the topic of the next chapter. It creates a hospitable space to welcome the real.

No pledge, no ed[ge] . . . ucation

The widespread knowledge-as-information orientation thwarts all knowing ventures, but perhaps most tragically it damages the knowing venture of college students. Most first-years arrive with a knowledge-as-information posture intact and unrecognized. Their parents may be the ones pledging the major financial investment. Young college students may be clueless about the responsible personal pledge that lies at the heart of any knowing venture. When they presume that all there is to knowledge is attending classes and collecting information, they are further tempted to pledge their energies in other activities besides the main act of the very knowing ventures for which they have come. They don't embrace the responsible commitment it takes to mine the strategic opportunity before them. And to that extent, they fail to be educated and to learn to know.

Reorienting our posture of knowing to loving-in-order-to-know targets this unfortunate situation, replacing it with the orientation most effective for knowing ventures. It drastically heightens the value of our investment and our productivity. This reorientation requires our responsible, sometimes risky, personal pledge.

Commitment, not curiosity

Any knowing venture requires the knower to take responsibility for it, to pledge him or herself to it. Commitment is the way we dispose ourselves toward the thing we want to know. We take a responsible, highly sophisticated, human, step of choice to bind ourselves in covenant with it. Commitment is different from curiosity, if we mean by curiosity an indifferent, uninvested, responsibility-free stance. (If by curiosity we mean a stance of wonder—that, of course, *is* good and important.)

Commitment to what you do not yet know

Never forget the wondrous fact that the knower pledges her or himself to what she or he does not yet know. The knowledge-as-information picture of knowing entirely misses this. It misses it because the only thing that counts as knowledge is clear information. But all knowing is coming to know what we do not yet know entirely. What's more, where reality and knowing are transformative, coming to know isn't going to be linear or additive. We can be clueless and be very close. We can be immensely informed and be very far away. The knowledge-as-information picture is blind to this as well. What it means is that the thing we do not yet know but pledge ourselves to know is not just a mere procedural step away. It's going to take something like a miracle. So it is going to take a pledge to invite it.

How is it even possible to pledge yourself to what you do not yet know? How is it possible to love it? As chapter 1 suggested, reality has in some way already beckoned and we have responded in wonder. We can have only a bare hint that something is there that is worth our loving pursuit. To pledge is to begin to respond. It is to decide to take the risk to move out into the dark to follow where it leads. To pledge is to say "I do" to the knowing venture.

Such a pledge requires the thing we talked about in the last chapter: a fundamental trust in the dynamic, generous, love-responsive faithfulness of reality. Yet a pledge is not a bargain, not a contract, not a condition. It has nothing stand-offish about it. It hopes; it does not presume. It commits, withholding nothing.

Pledging your allegiance to what you do not yet know is enormously risky. Until you get used to doing this, it can be terrifying. When you do get used to it, it can become the kind of risk we enjoy and embrace as adventure.

What we pledge

What is it that we pledge? We pledge to give ourselves to the yet-to-be-known, and to consent to its being. We pledge to take the risk to follow something that may prove not to be there, something that may prove to be way different from what we imagine. We accept the prospect that others might think us foolish—that we might prove to be foolish.

We pledge to do what we find it takes to live our lives on the terms of the yet-to-be-known. We must attend more and more to the thing we pursue, to see how to shape our approach so as to invite it. We must develop the attentiveness to see and embrace the world from the perspective of the desired thing. We pledge to stick to it.

We pledge ourselves to the work it will take. We must count the cost. We must change our behavior, stopping some activities and beginning others. We may need to acquire a skill or two. That takes an investment of time and money and sheer determination. It may require these things in daunting amounts. It does take amassing information, sometimes massive amounts. But amassing information becomes richly meaningful in this larger context, when it is no longer defining knowing. Instead, we are striving to indwell the information, to get it inside us so it becomes part of us. We are not after information so much as its significance. We indwell amassed information as part of striving to live life on the terms of the yet-to-be-known.

We pledge also to open ourselves to the transformation and to the new reality that the yet-to-be-known will bring us. We must be willing to have it change us, without specifying or holding at arm's length the change we will undergo. Or if we do specify this we must see that we are limiting the nature of the relationship we will have with it over time. This is often quite legitimate: Growing in knowing ourselves in relation to the world and to others means being strategically selective in our personal investments, attending to our own gifts and trusting the diverse gifts of others in our team. It means pledge-like guarding of other commitments we have already assumed.

But for each of us there are a few things it is as if we are designed to pursue. Each of us has a distinct, signature way of seeing and loving the world. It yields signature things that we notice and that prompt our wonder. It shapes our calling. One of these personally noticed things probably lies half-hidden in the knowing venture you now embrace. And to move toward it, you pledge openness to its changing you. Here is where we get another peek at the living dynamism of reality. When we come to know we and reality change in some way. This is both humbling and joyous.

Another dimension of our pledge is that we pledge to give space and welcome to the yet-to-be-known. We accord it space for truthful self-disclosure. We want, really, to know the thing as it is, not the thing as our preconceived notions expect it to be. If we mistakenly emphasize our expectations we will get what we expect, but we will prevent truth.

We must make a careful distinction here. Sometimes putting words on a thing is just what invites it into being. But these are words we have let the reality itself suggest to us, or words we have guessed at, and the reality has suddenly, transformatively confirmed. "That's not a rock, Jim; that's a *being*—a *mother*," we can imagine Dr. Leonard "Bones" McCoy, the Enterprise's irascible doctor, pronouncing in surprise. This is the kind of wording that we want to practice: the kind that offers a chance for the yet-to-be-known to show itself truthfully.

But on the other side, we must pledge to apply our categories tentatively, listening always around the edges of them, so to speak, to gauge whether the fit is apt. A knowledge-as-information view of knowledge can make no sense of this essential and everyday human capacity. With the help of SFI in chapter 4, we can.

Trust: the other side of pledge

The other side of pledge, we can see, must be trust. The *Little Manual* has already called for trust regarding our orientation in knowing. The knowing venture calls us to trust ourselves to something we seek to know, to trust ourselves to its developments, to trust ourselves to a reality that is relationally responsive and generous, to trust ourselves to relationship, to trust ourselves to carefully chosen authoritative guides and to companions on the journey, to trust ourselves in the knowing venture. It also involves the yet-to-be-known in some way coming to trust *us*.

Pledge and trust together display the normative and the relational dimensions of a knowing venture. A well-respected philosopher of education makes the point that the word "truth" is related to the old word "troth." Troth means a solemn pledge of faithfulness in relationship, as in a marriage vow. This link powerfully underscores that pledge and trust are the central nerve of knowing.

In your knowing venture, your pledge is your decision to buy in or sign on. You may have made the decision to make an investment, or to join a team, to take up a venture. Pledge permeates the world of business. In art or design, you give yourself to a vision. You decide to try something, pledging to follow where it leads. In community service you give yourself to seeing and hearing needs and potential, pledging to serve as you are able, to lend your expertise to addressing and developing what you see and hear.

In a college classroom, although it is rarely ceremonially observed or even noticed, there must be a moment where a student says, "Yes! I do hereby accept this challenge. I give myself to it and to what it requires. I pledge to trust the guidance of the professor, to guard my time to make a priority of the work that it will take to gain the skills and carry out the assignments. I pledge to listen deeply and humbly to the text. I pledge faithful support to my classmates. I pledge to be patient. What's more, I pledge to allow myself to be transformed into what I am not yet. I pledge my troth to the reality I do not yet know. Where no pledge takes place, no education transpires."

Your knowing venture invites your pledge. From this day forward you enter into pilgrimage.

Exercises for your knowing venture

1. Identify the dimensions of pledge that your knowing venture is calling for. Discuss these and express them in a form that you can commit to. Specifically:

    a. In what way are you pledging your consent to the being of the yet-to-be-known?

    b. In what way are you risking the criticism of others?

    c. What things can you identify that will count as learning to live life on the terms of the yet-to-be-known?

    d. In what ways can you grow your attentiveness to the yet-to-be-known and to the world in light of it?

    e. What work, activities, skills, time, and money investment do you pledge to the yet-to-be-known?

    f. What information will you need to commit yourself to amass and indwell?

2. What does it look like to pledge yourself to the potential personal transformation this discovery might afford you?

3. Do you need to set boundaries on your self-giving to this venture? If so, what are they?

4. What does it look like to pledge yourself to a new reality that this discovery might afford you and others?

5. What does it look like to pledge hospitable space to the yet-to-be-known, to welcome its truthful self-disclosure?

6. Identify the trust involved in your knowing venture. Identify the trust that the yet-to-be-known must place in you.

7. Identify the risks involved in these pledges. What is a responsible risk, and what risks serve as warning lights?

8. Discuss how your pledges heighten the effectiveness of your knowing venture.

9. Discuss how it might not help your knowing venture if someone else takes the pledge for you, or requires the pledge of you. What can be done in these situations?

10. For fun, and to underscore the act of pledging, devise a ceremony of pledging yourself(selves) in these ways in your knowing venture.

CHAPTER 3

Invitation

KNOWING IS CULTIVATING A relationship as you would with another person. Knowing is "interpersonlike," we might say. If so, then good knowing practice involves relating to what we want to know the way we relate to another person. We don't demand or presume or help ourselves. Success depends on the other as much as it does on ourselves, and we can't force what the other can give. In fact, if we do we don't get to know the other as it is, really. The other retreats and hides. What it surrenders, when forced, is not itself.

So we should see ourselves as *inviting the real*, welcoming the yet-to-be-known. And to do that calls for proper interpersonal behavior. We can think of this as epistemological etiquette, or great knowing practices.

The practices of inviting the real apply obviously to the venture of coming to know another person. But they apply to any knowing venture. And these practices might not look like what we usually think knowing involves. We usually think it involves dispassionate information collection. This is the knowledge-as-information approach. But once we reorient to inviting the real, even collecting information becomes meaningful and passionate, because it is part (not all) of a larger vision of loving in order to know. Collecting information, once embedded in this vision, and approached in a certain way, is the faithful practice of attending carefully that invites the real.

We have already talked about love and pledge. These defining postures frame the knowing venture and anchor inviting the real. But in this chapter we examine other dimensions of inviting the real. We flesh out what great knowing looks like and what it involves.

We'll talk here about ourselves as knowers: about readiness to know and how we comport ourselves in knowing. We'll consider effective strategies in knowing. We'll note what sustaining the relationship involves, because these too are great knowing practices. But we'll talk further about these in Part 2.

Readiness to know: maturity in love

Great knowing ventures are made great partly by what their knowers bring to the venture. What they bring are themselves. And the more readied the knower is, the more the knower brings, and the better the venture.

Readiness to know is essentially a matter of maturity in love. This doesn't mean that knowing doesn't come to people not yet matured as lovers. It does mean that maturation improves knowing. Actually, knowing ventures themselves mature us in love. For knowing anything is also knowing yourself. And maturing involves knowing and being known. Incidentally, this is why we ought to associate wisdom with grey hair.

There are two ways to get at this maturity in love that invites the real. This discussion intertwines them. One is the idea that it takes another person or persons to help us be the persons we are. The other is the idea that it takes developing fully as human persons in all four dimensions of humanness. Both are involved often in any healing path we might need to take on the way to maturity. These two interweave, and knowing ventures can be seen to interweave with them also. Love drives knowing; knowing matures us into full personhood and readiness to know.

The loving gaze that makes us persons

To be human is indeed to be a uniquely complex sort of being. Some philosophers have rightly argued that to be a person is to be a person in communion with another person. It takes at least two to be one. When we think of ourselves, our perception of ourselves is always incomplete. We spend our lives, every day of them, considering who we are. No other animal does this! The best handles we get on who we are are always the good pronouncements of other persons regarding ourselves. And it is in the loving gaze of caring, significant others in our lives that we find ourselves. In our self-awareness we actually grow into that gaze, and into those pronouncements, as we take them to heart. This is how we mature in love.

The Loving Gaze of the Other

The healing path

All of us have had really bad experiences of other people and at the hands of life. We have been cursed or shamed or violated or betrayed. An approach to knowing that understands the significance of maturing in love also understands the wreckage that betrayal brings and how it hinders knowing. If trust is critical to knowing, distrust impedes it. But the journey that is our lives must involve seeking a path of healing, finding a way to rise above such hurt and to transmute it into greater strength, hope, love, and trust. This healing path, as one author/therapist calls it, itself is a maturation of love that makes us better at knowing ventures.

The Void—an important dimension of humanness

One counselor/philosopher calls the threat or possibility of non-being, the Void. Being dealt a curse threatens our being. Many things besides curses and betrayal give us a sense of the Void, however: a brush with death or fear, depression or danger, an uncomfortable situation, even boredom. But a sense of the possibility of not being need not result from curse or hardship. It can be simply a felt need, a felt absence, a felt "I might not be." That means that sensing the Void lies at the heart of wonder, and of gratitude. The Void need not be evil or hardship. But given our proclivity to maintain control by coping in a two-dimensionally human way means that often it is the Void as threat that alone breaks through.

We all experience the Void in some form or other. It is inevitable because it is true: we *might not exist.* And a sense of the Void is not something we go looking for. It comes unbidden from outside of us.

We often hear that humanness involves only two dimensions: ourselves and our situation. Humanness is successfully coping with our situation. But the Void—the deep realization that we might not exist, that we need something, someone, beyond ourselves—is actually an important third dimension of our humanness. And I say it again: we cannot manufacture it; the Void comes unbidden, perhaps graciously, from outside of us. We cannot manufacture it, but we can do right by it, and we can cultivate it.

The healing path requires that we embrace the possibility of nonbeing that hurtful experiences involve. If we deny the threat, or resign ourselves to it, we aren't doing the healing thing with the Void. The healing thing is to admit our need truthfully and cry out for deliverance. This is what happens when we come to the end of ourselves and start to look in hope beyond ourselves for help. We open ourselves to what we cannot manufacture and cannot presume to deserve. We open ourselves to what can only come graciously: the possibility of new being.

But this is the sort of thing we must do whether we have been hurt or not. A responsible engagement of the Void lies at the heart of our maturing into full humanness and personhood. In fact, understanding the might-not-be of gift is essential to inviting reality in good knowing.

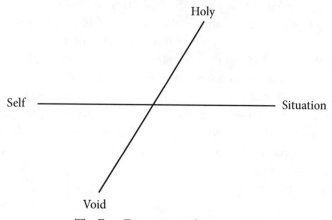

The Four Dimensions of Humanness

The fourth dimension of humanness

In the Void, we must cry out in hope for the gracious deliverance and inbreaking of new being. This is a key act of inviting the real. It's how coming to personal readiness to know is itself a knowing venture. We begin to move from deep hurt and need, choosing to move beyond shutting down, to reach out beyond ourselves, to the possibility of new being, and invite its gracious involvement.

The gracious possibility of new being is the fourth dimension of humanness. The psychologist/philosopher from whom the *Little Manual* draws this analysis calls this fourth dimension, the Holy. To be fully human, we must embrace this. It, too, comes from beyond us. It is not something we can manufacture. It is something we consent to welcome.

To have developed all four dimensions of humanness is to be a person who can give him or herself in love. This is the maturation in love that invites the real. It opens out into healthy relationship and great knowing ventures.

The four dimensions of humanness and the knowing venture

The four dimensions of humanness also factor into all knowing ventures. Knowing begins with a sense of wonder, notice, and puzzlement. This is a sense that something might not be, a sense of something that we do not have or understand. The sense of a problem that needs solving is an experience of the Void. Moving along the trajectory of coming to know involves our inviting the real. Reality coming in newness is the fourth dimension of our humanness. This is how knowing ventures, in turn, grow us as persons, maturing us as knowers. For coming to know itself is the inbreaking of the possibility of new being.

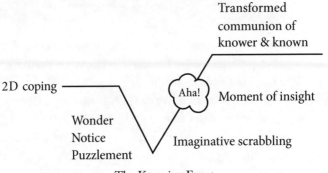

The Knowing Event

Melding persons in communion, the loving regard of the other, and the fourth dimension

We can return to the first idea of persons in communion and superimpose it on the development of the fourth dimension of humanness. To be held in regard by another person, to see that regard reflected in a gaze or in caring words of commendation, is the communion that calls us to be fully persons. It is the gracious possibility of new being that fulfills our humanness.

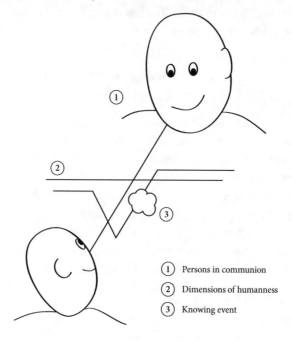

(1) Persons in communion
(2) Dimensions of humanness
(3) Knowing event

If you have or are considering a relationship with God, this is where it ties in profoundly. God is the ultimate other person who comes into our Void and delivers us in gracious love. We can live joyously and freely and for him. We live fully in his delighted regard. It matures us in the best way to be selves who give in love. But the regard of ordinary human persons is also critical to our full humanness. It is right that people often connect the love of God with the love of ordinary human persons. The human, touchable face radiating a gaze a love—that is a reality apart! It forms us into ourselves.

"Love is the gift of the self"

Personal wholeness requires another, another who gives reciprocally. This is no mercenary gift "exchange"! To be a true act of giving it must be gracious, expecting nothing in return—no strings attached. True mutuality in giving is never tit-for-tat, but rather it is gracious overture and gracious response. Friendship is a continual mutual self-giving. Personal wholeness comes when we accept the gracious prospect of new being and become able to give ourselves in love. Mutual gift giving is the being-in-communion that full humanness is.

A recent Roman Catholic pope/philosopher has argued that a person cannot fully find himself except through the gift of the self that is love. Love is at the core of all things; it makes sense that it is at the core of who we are. And maturing in love strategically invites the real in our knowing ventures. If love is the gift of the self, and we love in order to know, then we give ourselves in order to know.

Readiness to know: presence

Maturation in love brings with it a sense of self that is hard to describe, but real and palpable. It is a sense of personal beauty or dignity. We can call it presence, or being there. It is being centered. It is being at peace. If knowing involves the self, the self that knows must be there, at home, present. This involves being okay with not being some other, including the thing that is the not-yet-known. Presence grants otherness to others. This is essential to healthy knowing and to productive teamwork in the process. Presence is being present to attend to the other without being threatened by it. It is being present to welcome hospitably the yet-to-be-known. Presence is readiness to know.

Our felt body sense

There is one big thing that this involves, something a knowledge-as-information mode utterly overlooks: our body. In presuming that knowledge is a mental activity we tend to think of our body strictly as a mindless container—an object. Of course, we understand that our senses take in information and our brains process it.

But we see this as mechanical. We actually think computers might duplicate how humans know.

But in fact we rely on our bodies, not as objects, but as *felt*. We don't merely plug in information if we are going to return a wicked tennis serve. We have to indwell and bodily feel that response. It's not enough to know what it is; we must know what it feels like in our bodies. It is not mindless processing of opaque information. This is our felt body sense. Our felt body sense is just what makes it that we feel our bodies to be our own.

Being at home, being present, centering, all involve felt body sense. They are being at home in our felt bodies. Again, this is hard to describe, but palpable and real. We can actually mark its absence or presence in others. And we can cultivate it in ourselves. Certain activities cultivate it well; other activities very much do not cultivate it. And the key thing about these activities seems to be that you *take them* to be cultivating your felt body sense. After all, thinking is a bodily activity, but if you pursue it in a disembodied way, it doesn't grow your felt body sense. On the other hand, athletics is a bodily activity, but if we pursue it as if our body is a machine, it doesn't grow our felt body sense. Yet if we can identify this felt body sense, then we can tap all bodily activity to hone it.

Learning to identify, care for, trust, and tap our felt body sense is a key to effective knowing ventures. Any body care has the potential to cultivate your felt body sense. This includes any skill that we learn, or activity we carry out, as well as any care we take for health and dignity. It includes rest and play. The particular activity need not directly connect to our specific knowing venture, although it may. Of course, the loving care of another that makes us human is something we receive bodily as felt.

One way that we tap our felt body sense in knowing involves relying on our "gut" for clues as we move forward into the half-darkness in our knowing venture. Often our body senses something before we can name what it is. We need to trust it. We don't trust it blindly; our felt body sense is not infallible. But we may develop its level of accuracy through training.

Cultivating our felt body sense can take the form of virtuosity in a physical skill. Virtuosity is a level of skill that allows artistry in our bodily sense and response. Virtuosity obviously contributes to creative, imaginative involvement in our knowing ventures.

Welcome

Inviting the real, then, includes maturing in love. Greatly beloved lovers make great knowers. They can bring to the knowing situation the kind of welcome that invites the real. Welcome is the key posture of a knower wooing the yet-to-be-known.

Welcome is a highly sophisticated act that only persons can bring to be. Welcome is a "let there be," a normative enactment. It is, by way of pronouncing it so, to extend hospitality. It is gracious consent to the being and presence of the yet-to-be-known other.

Hospitality, as one well-known spiritual leader has defined it, involves creating a safe space into which the stranger may come and become a friend. It isn't an empty space; the host is there. But it is a space. It is a space that accords dignity and liberty to the other. It involves boundaries to protect the space, but no boundaries in the space.

Welcome can't guarantee the very thing it looks to do. So it risks rejection. It is made to depend on the response of the other. It honors that response.

In the welcoming space the host must be disposed toward the other, and at the other's disposal. The host must be there, but welcome is not about the host. Respect, humility, attentiveness, obedience to the other's desires, and patience, all characterize the good host. All these are gestures of welcome that furnish the hospitable space. So they are important practices to invite the real.

Comportment that invites the real

Our comportment in knowing ventures must be actively receptive in these ways. We respect what we want to know, treating it as having worth and being worth knowing, as other than ourselves. We comport ourselves humbly, deferring to its agency in our epistemic relationship. We attend to it, listening deeply to understand. We act promptly to accommodate its desires to the best of our understanding and ability. We exercise patience, which is the hospitable space of time for free expression and becoming. This is good comportment in our knowing venture.

Strategies to invite the real

We can gently distinguish these next practices from those of our comportment. These are more a matter of strategy. They involve active, savvy choices we make as knowers, which make good sense if we want to know.

Strategy 1: Choosing wise guides

A key strategy, especially early on, is to choose wise guides. We should choose people who are strategically qualified to help us. They expertly know something we need to know in our knowing venture. We should choose guides who also love what they know. They should be excited about it, delighted in it. If possible, we should choose guides who also care about us. Wise guides—expert and humbly caring—can be key members of our team in our venture to know. They can also serve as significant others who evoke our personal maturation in love.

A guide is only as effective as our decision to trust and to submit to that guide. We make a responsible choice to trust what they say even when we do not understand or agree. We cannot be suspicious or noncommittal about this. We have to be willing wholeheartedly to try out what they recommend. Apart from this that guide cannot help, and our investment does not pay off. Submission and trust are not the same as mindless compliance. They don't actually even require agreement. They involve another critically important, sophisticatedly human, covenantal "let there be." They involve free personal consent. Submission and trust aren't always comfortable. But they are necessary to knowing.

The legitimate and necessary trust of authoritative guides is not something that the typical knowledge-as-information vision of knowing even sees, let alone admits the value of. But it is not hard to recognize that no knowing ever occurs without it—even for people who deny their dependence on such guides.

What authoritative guides supply us is normative. They give us a "this is the way you should look at this." Authoritative guides tell us what we ought to see and how to see it. It is a wondrous thing that in this process they are not helping us make up our own reality. Rather, they are helping us see what is already there. Submission to wise guides opens the world to us.

This doesn't mean we are locked into the exact words of the guides. The goal is not to be them or parrot them. (This would not be maturity in love, the thing we need to be great knowers.) What we do with what they give us is to grow to indwell the guides' maxims with our own virtuosity, artfully engaging the world from them.

Strategy 2: Placing ourselves where reality is likely to show up

A second key strategy to invite the real is to place ourselves where what we are looking for is most likely to show itself. It would seem that this simple strategy requires almost nothing of us. Yet it is an act of self-giving, of respect and humility, disposing ourselves toward the yet-to-be-known. Choosing a wise guide is itself putting ourselves in the place knowing shows up. There are additional ways we do it, as when we put ourselves behind a telescope when we want to see Jupiter, or position ourselves strategically along a parade route. And of course, if our mission lies on the other side of the world, putting ourselves in the place reality is likely to show up will be costly indeed.

Strategy 3: Active listening

Third, we need to attend and listen actively. Attentiveness and listening are already ways we hospitably welcome the real. But they also have a positive, active side. Our attentiveness can actually prove creative, bringing to be what is not yet. It can bring the real to be itself as it gives itself to us. Our listening can be the catalyst that evokes the story waiting to be told. We make a costly mistake if we take listening to be mere passive reception of indifferent data. We miss out on the good strategy of conferring the dignity that invests in the real that we want to know. It is important to see that attentiveness dynamically engages the real. It shows how knowing is an unfolding, dynamic relationship. It shows how our knowing venture shapes reality.

Remember that this is just what occurs when we mature as persons in the loving gaze of the other. The other has invited our reality to grow to be more fully itself.

A fourth strategy to invite the real is indwelling. Indwelling involves empathetically putting ourselves inside the thing we want to know and taking it inside us. The next chapter explores indwelling more fully.

Additionally, the dimensions of sustaining a relationship between knower and known themselves invite the real. So the topics in chapter 7 of the *Little Manual*, dance and communion, round out the epistemological etiquette.

Inviting the real in our knowing venture

We should see our knowing venture as born of wonder and love and constituted in pledge. In it we extend hospitable welcome to invite the real. We cultivate ourselves as knowers in the maturity of love that readies us for knowing, maturing to give ourselves in love as candidates to romance the real. We comport ourselves as gracious hosts, in humility, attentiveness, and obedient response. We strategize in our choice of guides. We seek out a vantage point to which the real may come. We cultivate active attentiveness and listening that evokes the real. And we seek to indwell and be indwelt by the yet-to-be-known.

The college years are all about maturation in love toward readiness to know. Any student can mark his or her progress semester by semester. College is also very much about choosing wise guides, about putting oneself in a place where reality is likely to show up, and about active listening. Welcoming the yet-to-be-known with respect, humility, patience, and attentiveness is what every good teacher and classroom must ensure and inculcate. In attending college, we are being intentional in practicing epistemological etiquette to invite the real.

But any business venture, artistic effort, or community service is advanced critically by personal maturation in love. The matured lover who can give the gift of self is the one who will invite reality best and healingly. Wisdom, savvy, artistry, innovation, and care grow deeply with this maturation. Any knowing venture, and any team venturing together, will be blessed with reality's fertile self-disclosure only as it ensures a welcoming space, in which respect, humility, patience, and attentive listening are practiced. Plus, it is easy to see that each sort of pursuit—business, art, athletics, design, community care, or human service—benefits from choosing wise guides and strategically locating ourselves to invite reality.

Thus far the pilgrimage to discovery.

Exercises for your knowing venture

1. As you consider your specific knowing venture what are some concrete examples of your practicing epistemological etiquette to invite the real? What are some practices you might adjust to invite it better?

2. Consider your own level of maturation as a person capable of giving yourself in love.

   a. Rate it on a scale of 1 to 10, where 1 is not at all mature and 10 is completely mature.

    b. List and describe some factors that contribute, positively or negatively, to where you are on this scale. Specifically, try to describe these in light of the four dimensions of humanness (especially the Void and the Holy) and the idea of persons—and the team—being formed in the noticing regard of a caring other.

    c. In light of this, what are some things you need to address or practices you need to cultivate?

    d. How does this bear on moving forward in your knowing venture?

3. Consider your maturity in love as a team.

    a. Rate it on a scale of 1 to 10, where 1 is not at all mature and 10 is completely mature.

    b. List and describe some factors that contribute, positively or negatively, to where you are on this scale. Specifically, try to describe these in light of the idea of the four dimensions of humanness (especially the Void and the Holy) and the idea of persons—and the team—being formed in the noticing regard of a caring other.

    c. In light of this, what are some things you need to address or practices you need to cultivate?

    d. How does this bear on moving forward in your knowing venture?

4. Identify the Void in your knowing venture. What is your sense of need that drives your inquiry?

5. List some ways that, in your knowing venture, you can exhibit presence.

6. In what ways does your knowing venture involve your felt body sense? How can you cultivate this?

7. In what way, in your knowing venture, can you welcome the yet-to-be-known? What effect does this have on your venture?

8. How may the following be cultivated in your knowing venture?

   a. Respect.

   b. Humility.

   c. Attentiveness.

   d. Obedience.

   e. Patience.

9. Identify authoritative guides for your knowing venture.

   a. For each, assess their qualifications, their love for their subject, and their care for you.

   b. Consider your own contribution of submission: Have you given your consent to them to be guided by them?

   c. Or if you find either that your guide candidates are not qualified or do not have your trust, what steps should you take to address this?

10. Discuss some examples of authoritative guides teaching us to see what is there and opening the world to us.

11. In your knowing venture, in what way are you placing yourself where the yet-to-be-known is likely to show up? In what way are you not doing this and need to revise your strategy?

12. Discuss some examples that show how inviting the real can actually help the reality you invite develop to be more itself. In what ways does your knowing venture have the prospect of doing this?

CHAPTER 4

Indwelling

INDWELLING INVOLVES EMPATHETICALLY PUTTING yourself inside the thing you want to know, and taking it inside you. Indwelling is a strategy to invite the real. Indwelling is what it looks like to give oneself in love in an effort to know. It is part of what welcome looks like, what trust looks like, and caring attentiveness.

And what indwelling looks like is this: relying on clues "subsidiarily" to shape a complex focal pattern. This chapter unpacks what this means. Here we introduce you to *subsidiary-focal integration*, or SFI. SFI is the concrete structure of any knowing. It is what loving in order to know looks like concretely. It makes a lot of practical sense of any knowing venture.

Knowledge-as-information can't make sense of coming to know

The common knowledge-as-information approach casts knowing as collecting information. It presumes that the information is entirely clear. All information can be verbally expressed in sentences. It just needs transferring, impersonally, from its impersonal source to us. No personal investment is involved. Information is what it is without our indwelling it.

But to anyone starting a knowing venture, it is obvious that what you do not yet know is neither verbalized nor clear. It is not impersonally transferable. It is obvious that a knowing venture requires personal investment and savvy. It's not an obvious linear process to go from not knowing to knowing. A knowing venture shows that the knowledge-as-information approach is not the best and most effective picture of knowing.

Once and for all, SFI will demonstrate why the knowledge-as-information epistemology is both false and damaging. Knowing is way more complex. Knowing is also way more freeingly human—suiting us as glove to hand, not reducing us to the automata we aren't. But understanding SFI not only makes sense of knowing ventures; it also winsomely woos us into them. We find ourselves rooted in knowing and rooted in the world. We find ourselves freed to the real adventure of knowing. And we become significantly better at it as we trust ourselves to the epistemic guidance of SFI.

Identifying the subsidiary that anchors the focal

In fact, as one philosopher puts it, no knowledge is ever wholly focal and explicit—even what we already know. This means that we don't focus on everything we know, and we can't put it all in words, all at the same time, or at any time. Anything we are focally aware of is rooted in an awareness that is not focal. Like an iceberg, actually most of our knowing—the most important part of our knowing—operates unseen below the surface of the focal, as subsidiary. The subsidiary outruns and anchors focal knowledge, and it makes it possible.

Right now we are attending to the ideas in this discussion. That's where our focus lies. We aren't actually focusing on these particular sentences and keystrokes, although we can't do without them. What we are doing with respect to the sentences is relying on them *subsidiarily*. We are aware of them, but it is not focal awareness; it is not subconscious, either. It is subsidiary awareness. We are indwelling the sentences subsidiarily. We are attending *from* them, not *to* them.

The subsidiary is what we indwell in all our knowing. Sentences of text offer only one example. Life is entirely full of examples of subsidiary-focal integration. It is really helpful to stop and think of some, and then to start to look at knowing as SFI. In fact, it is way easier to get the feel of SFI from examples than it is to read and follow a written description of it. So this chapter makes sense more easily as we think it through in connection with a knowing we know well. Eventually, we want to see our specific knowing venture as exemplifying SFI. Doing that will enhance our effort to know.

So, for example: Every time we notice something, picking out an object or pattern, we are focusing on that thing and relying subsidiarily on an array of other things. We rely subsidiarily on background and surroundings. We rely subsidiarily on our felt body sense. We rely on authoritative guides in the form of mothers, coaches, traditions, theoretical frameworks. That means that the simplest perception involves SFI: this cup beside me, that flower vase over there. But so does the most theoretical claim: Chemical elements conform to the pattern of the Periodic Table. This patient has cancer. Reality is personlike.

Any skill—and just about everything we do is skill-related— involves SFI: riding a bike, driving a car, handwriting, crafting a violin, playing a violin, long-snapping a football, offering spiritual direction, doing philosophy—we could go on interminably. All involve relying subsidiarily on clues to focus on and sustain a pattern.

Subsidiaries can't simultaneously be focal. We can't attend from them and to them at the same time. At the time we rely on them we can't fully specify them, and they can't be put into words. They are tacit rather than explicit.

Subsidiaries are neither subjective nor private, although they are the working out of responsible personal commitment. Subsidiaries are neither mystical nor magical, although they cannot be simultaneously indwelled and verbally expressed and although they can never be wholly expressed. They are palpable, rooted in our embodiment and rooting us in the world, concretely enacting the guidance of guiding words. They are palpably felt, the way our bodies are palpably felt to be our own. That palpable feel makes the subsidiary wonderfully ordinary. Reading and understanding involves the wonderful ordinariness of relying on sentences to attend to meaning. Riding a bike involves the wonderfully ordinary subsidiary, skilled, artful, felt-body sense of keeping your balance. Indwelling subsidiaries often has the wonderful sense of being at home—in ourselves and in the world.

And in contrast to the body-marginalizing, indifferent, and arbitrary "feel" of a knowledge-as-information approach, subsidiary awareness locates the responsible, personed, knower centrally as the embodied anchor of all her or his knowings.

Integration

All knowledge and knowing has a "from-to" structure. It has two connected levels, the focal and the subsidiary. Each is what it is in that relation to the other. We are aware of the subsidiaries as they bear on the focal pattern. The pattern makes sense of the subsidiaries. The relationship between focal and subsidiary is like whole to part.

The relationship between subsidiaries and focus is not linear. It is not like you can add up the subsidiaries and derive the focal. (Addition would require the subsidiaries to be focal—that is, no longer subsidiary.) Staring at an *s*, or at the word "subsidiary," itself in no way produces or guarantees understanding the word—although there may be guidelines we can indwell (subsidiarily) to figure out how to do this.

If anything, it seems as if the relationship goes the other way around: the focal pattern makes sense of the subsidiaries. But that relationship isn't linear or deductive either. The focal pattern is not reducible to the subsidiaries. There seems to be no necessary core set of subsidiaries. The relationship is transformative: the pattern transforms what it involves subsidiarily. The relationship between subsidiary clues and focal pattern is one of *integration*—an imaginative synthesizing of a transforming, three-dimensional pattern.

For example, we can think of how we make meaning of a text, working from a wide, and sometimes varying, array of subsidiaries. We can read all kinds of fonts. We can make sense of misspelled words, even of sentences with missing words or letters. An expert cyclist could probably keep riding in all kinds of terrain, with various parts of the bike or his body damaged or even missing (perish the thought!). As we indwell the subsidiaries, we creatively integrate to a sustained focal pattern.

Integration is the way humans know. Humans hold subsidiary and focal together in the action of integration. We may say that the "glue" that is integration is a responsible human reach outward toward the world.

Integration is both active and passive. We actively shape clues into a pattern; and we passively submit to the pattern. A human knower actively, responsibly relies on clues to shape a transformative pattern. Integration is the human gesture of knowing. The knower personally, responsibly commits, disposing him or herself to the foray. The knower riskily, creatively scrabbles to indwell clues to achieve a focal pattern. It takes love and commitment.

But integration is receptive, as we will see in the next part of this *Little Manual*. This is no bare fabrication. We will find our risky venture engages and unlocks a reality in a way that surprises and changes us.

It takes a rider to ride a bike. But once underway, bike riding unlocks the world. It takes a trained radiologist to see a green stick fracture. But such a diagnosis brings healing.

SFI and coming to know

All knowing is subsidiary-focal integration. We rely on subsidiary clues to creatively shape a focal pattern. But how does SFI factor in to our coming to know in the first place? Coming to know proves to be a process of moving from looking *at* to looking *from* in order see transformatively *beyond.*

The knowing venture we are undertaking is a coming-to-know. We identify in it the telltale dimensions of SFI. Doing so will make us more effective at it. No matter the field of inquiry, we'll know better what knowing is and how to go about it.

Before the outset of our venture, we are looking *at* an apparently disconnected, meaningless array of particular items. Yet our love- and pledge-motivated wonder, our unspecifiable sense of a deeper meaning and of future prospects, our inexplicable excitement, our puzzlement over a problem, hint of a hidden reality. This, our already longing and loving to know, is itself signposting, and thus becoming subsidiary to a farther, half-hidden focus.

We enter a calculus class at the outset of a term. The professor writes inscrutable hieroglyphics on the board. No amount of staring at them, or even writing them down and memorizing them, in itself is knowledge. But we cry out: "What does this mean? I want to know!" Already these expressions signal that a shift is underway. We are giving ourselves to the pilgrimage to insight. We are drawn by a tantalizing hope.

Now what we must do is find a way to shift from attending to particulars focally, to indwelling them subsidiarily as clues. That shift is not automatic. The items attended to focally and the same items indwelt subsidiarily might as well be two different things. It takes a kind of creative scrabbling to pull this off—an imaginative casting about. You keep your eye, focally, on what you do not yet know, while you cast about subsidiarily for how to indwell subsidiarily what is before you. This is a dynamic struggle, one that can unfold over a short or a lengthy period of time. It is the creative, artistic act—whether making a painting or designing a ball park. It is also the act of discovery. It is the act of learning. It is how we come to ride a bike or acquire any skill. It is how we solve a mystery.

In the process of coming to know, subsidiaries work like clues in a detective mystery. A sleuth may sense the significance of a certain occurrence or item. He or she might be entirely mistaken. But, if it is significant, the sleuth has then to discover the way in which it is significant. In fact, the sleuth must entrust her or himself to clues that she or he has not yet even noticed focally. The sleuth has to scrabble subsidiarily, with an eye on the yet-to-be-known, to indwell the clues, to find how they bear on the as-yet-unidentified pattern. Only after the mystery is solved are the clues actually confirmed as clues. But by then you no longer need to rely on them to uncover the pattern. You continue to rely on them subsidiarily as a meaningful part of the pattern.

Three dimensions of subsidiaries:
body, guides, situation

We draw subsidiaries from three dimensions. First, from our felt body sense. Our felt body sense is *felt* precisely because it is subsidiary. We are always indwelling our bodies as they bear on a further reality. If, as we play a piano piece, we were to shift our focus from our performance to our thumbs, the performance would grind to halt.

We also extend our bodies to indwell any tools we have developed the skill to use. When hammering we attend from the hammer, subsidiarily indwelt, to the performance of roofing a house. The same is true for the cars we indwell as we drive.

We draw subsidiaries, secondly, from any normative guides or frameworks we are relying on to make sense of the situation. We indwell normative visions and maxims the way we indwell tools. We meld them with our felt body sense. Our very epistemology is one such normative framework we indwell.

Subsidiary indwelling makes great sense of what we do when we adopt a guide or an interpretative framework. This is an act of trust and submission, rather than a matter of indifferently amassing already lucid information. By now it should be obvious why this is. Information is focal. The maxims of wise guides themselves aren't exhaustively focal. Authoritative guides express what they hold in a stance or belief that is itself rich with subsidiaries. And what you want to do with normative maxims is indwell them subsidiarily. When you do this, the way they come to expression is not in rigidly exact compliance but rather (eventually) in artful virtuosity that uniquely displays what you as an individual bring to it.

The third source of subsidiaries is the situation itself, the place of our puzzled inquiry. It's the very thing we want to make sense of. We have to find a way to empathetically put ourselves inside the yet-to-be-known—to indwell it. We are probing to make sense of the situation, to connect the dots. The puzzle has originated because there are things in our situation that don't add up. So we are seeking a fresh, creative way to make sense of them.

Every knowing must involve all three dimensions of sub-sidiaries—our felt body sense, our indwelt normative guides and maxims, and our growing sense of the situation. They factor into our coming to know, also. Our journey of coming to know may have been prompted by one of these before the others. It can be any one of them: a wonder-filled, puzzling situation, a felt body sense that reality is different from what we may have thought, or inscrutable words of a would-be guide. Then, in the pilgrimage of coming to know, we navigate by spiraling from one to the other and to the third and back again. Words, world, felt body sense: we scrabble forward in one sector, and then take it into another to see if it resonates and if it evokes further insight. Eventually these will come together transformatively.

Analysis, training, practice, editing: temporarily focusing on subsidiaries

Knowing involves relying on subsidiaries. The plan is to rely on them to focus on a transformative pattern. Coming to know involves shifting from attending *to* to attending *from*. But subsidiaries themselves may need temporary focal attention. We often need to revert to attending *to* what we usually attend *from*. It is important to cultivate this reversion. But we must cultivate it as provisional and temporary.

A couple great examples of this are golfing and playing the piano. Golfers regularly visit the driving range to practice their technique. Pianists take lessons and practice, practice, practice. Practice involves attending focally to what we subsidiarily indwell in the performance. Practice identifies and fixes mistakes and enables expertise and virtuosity to grow. Other examples include study—say, of a new language—and editing and revising a paper. All schooling is helpfully seen in part as this temporary attentiveness to what is meant to be subsidiary.

Subsidiaries can operate without our focal awareness. Also, our integrations creatively orchestrate more than we need or realize in the way of subsidiaries. As a result of these things, we can be sustaining an integrative pattern without realizing that our subsidiary awareness has been in part mistaken or inadequate. Additionally, we can have been operating on automatic pilot. This renders our integrative pattern vulnerable to disintegration under unanticipated scrutiny or threat. Positively, our subsidiary awareness can be rendered expert by temporary attention. Its range and capacity can be expanded greatly. We can cultivate this temporary analysis as a caring, nurturing attentiveness.

Since knowing involves relying on subsidiary awareness to shape a focal pattern, whenever we focus on subsidiaries, we temporarily lose that focal pattern. Additionally, it is important to realize that when we "focus on subsidiaries," what we focus on is not the item *as subsidiary*. A hammer examined and a hammer swung might as well be two different things. To behold an *s* is not the same thing as to hiss like a snake.

So focusing on subsidiaries can be uncomfortable, disconcerting, unnatural, and risky. We would rather play the game or the music than practice the way we know we should. We would rather write than edit. Also, when we look *at* what we generally confidently look *from* the very integrative pattern we desire can evaporate into thin air. Attending to what we naturally indwell— such as our bodies—can feel unnatural. Finally we risk never again being able to reintegrate to the pattern, let alone improving our grasp of it by our temporary shift of attention.

We also risk embracing a faulty epistemology. The knowledge-as-information approach is just a fixation on analysis, a rendering of subsidiaries permanently focal. It enshrines focal information as the paradigm of knowledge. Apart from a gracious reorientation, there is no linear way back to subsidiaries as subsidiaries. Ironically, this fixation on information and analysis is in fact functioning subsidiarily!

So what we are doing here in this *Little Manual* is itself an example of a temporary analysis of what is more naturally subsidiary. For most of us, our defective subsidiary epistemic orientation has operated unnoticed and unexamined. The *Little Manual* is working to draw our subsidiary orientation to our attention so we can revise it and reindwell it with virtuosity. It is to be expected that the effort at first feels uncomfortable and risky. But for the reasons already noted, it is just the thing to make us better at all our knowing ventures.

The key to success in temporary analysis is twofold. First: we must remember it is temporary. Focal analysis is not knowledge. Successfully returning to subsidiary indwelling to looking from our practices and skills and analyses to their meaningful integrative bearing on the world—*that* is knowing.

Second: we must never lose sight of the goal. We must intersperse analysis with reintegration. We should keep close to others who can lift our eyes afresh to our hope. Doing these things amounts to a practice that we must attend to in order to indwell artfully. As we grow in it, we can trust ourselves to it.

Acquiring any skill in the first place involves this temporary focus on what will become subsidiary, as does any effort to come to know. Every knowing venture begins from outside the venture. But the pilgrimage to knowing often involves moving back and forth between attending *from* and attending *to*. The overarching journey toward insight includes repeated returns to attending to what we want to rely on. Being intentional about what can be a rhythmical to and fro in analysis and synthesis ups our effectiveness in knowing ventures, and it drives us along the path of our pilgrimage.

The telltale discomfort
on the verge of a breakthrough

All knowing is subsidiary-focal integration—SFI. Every knowing venture involves scrabbling to indwell certain things, known and unknown, subsidiarily as clues, guided by the distant star of something we long to know, to unlock a transformative pattern that resoundingly makes sense of our half-blind efforts.

The effort takes place over time. It is an unfolding journey—a pilgrimage. It is a journey that calls for our responsible, active investment. It is a journey of submission to invite the active self-disclosure of a real we dimly understand. Submitting to relying on clues subsidiarily invites the real. We seek integration to a qualitatively superior pattern. Our unfolding journey toward the yet-to-be-known may be studded by one small insightful integration, and then another, and then another.

The journey isn't always comfortable. For us to attain the integrative pattern, we have to let go of our focal grasp of the items before us. We cannot settle for them as knowledge. If we do, our knowing venture is doomed. So it's as if we bury a seed in the ground, dead to all appearances. That is the pledge-like self-giving that invites the real. That integrative shift isn't linear. It takes a logical leap.

On the verge of a breakthrough we can be fretful and uneasy. It isn't comfortable. What is going on is that we are no longer at home in our "old world," and we have not yet reached or been assured of a new one. Also, our felt body sense can be further along to our discovery than our thinking is. This puts parts of our self in conflict. We can learn, with experience, to be okay with our discomfort, in hope that it signals an impending breakthrough to insight. But even in this discomfort, our knowing venture moves forward in the hope of epiphany, and of the gracious gift of the real.

Exercises for your knowing venture

1. List as many examples of SFI as you can think of, from all corners of life.

2. If you have access to one, do a Magic Eye 3D puzzle. If you do not use reading a book as a similar case. Talk about how you shift from looking *at* the page to looking *from* the page to see the pattern. What do you learn about the experience of SFI?

3. Choose one of the examples you gave in #1. Identify in it the three dimensions of clues—felt body, normative framework or guide, and features of the situation.

4. How do you see SFI involved in your specific knowing venture? What does SFI suggest regarding how to go about it more effectively?

5. What are some items you are currently focusing on that you may need to shift to indwell subsidiarily in search of an integrative pattern? What are some concrete strategies of indwelling you might develop?

6. In your knowing venture, what are some subsidiaries that you may need temporarily to focus on and revise? How can you go about this? What are some subsidiaries with respect to which you can build a virtuosity that will help you in your knowing venture?

7. As you progress in your knowing venture how is the story unfolding? Identify periods of frustration and feeling out of kilter. How does it help to set these in the larger picture of indwelling and SFI?

PART II

Gift

CHAPTER 5

Encounter

W E ENDED THE LAST chapter of the first part of this *Little Manual* identifying a logical leap. Indwelling, scrabbling to climb into clues in a subsidiary way, is a bit like taking a plunge. We give ourselves in loving pledge to pilgrimage in the half dark, navigating by a dimly understood, half-hidden star. We are giving ourselves, and at that point we have no guarantee of eventual light. And, in fact, there is no guaranteed link between subsidiary and focal.

But our struggling to indwell the clues in a way that invites the real is itself a strategy to invite the real. And then, although there is no guarantee, we may find ourselves graciously blessed with integration—with insight and understanding.

Aha!

When an integration happens we can experience an "aha!" moment. What we experience in the "aha!" is the requisite shift from focally looking at particulars to subsidiarily looking from them. The puzzling particulars that preoccupied us have moved from our focal awareness to our subsidiary awareness. They have moved from opaque to transparent, opening up a further vista and allowing "in-sight."

Oh! I see it! I get it! Eureka! Epiphany! This is the moment of insight, a breakthrough. The light bulb goes on. The penny drops. Light dawns. We have arrived. These expressions signal the moment of discovery, the artistic creation, the business or design breakthrough, the getting of a skill such as balancing redox equations or keeping your balance on a bike. This shift need not be momentary, but it may be multiple moments. Or sometimes the light dawns slowly, almost imperceptibly. We wake up one morning and find that we are in a different place.

We all use these expressions. But since we have been stuck in the knowledge-as-information mode we have not seen that they indicate how knowing works. The knowledge-as-information approach hasn't recognized this integrative shift that lies at the heart of the knowing event. It hasn't occurred to us to shape our knowing by its guidance, or to invite it in love and pledge.

What we sense in the moment of insight and what it says about knowing

An epiphany is a great feeling. We feel a sense of happy conviction that our integration is right, or on the right track, and that it changes everything. We feel suddenly connected with all that up until now felt opaque: our body, the normative maxims of authoritative guides, the situation we did not yet understand. The feeling is registering a shift in our felt body sense. It counts as our coming to understand the guidance we have received. And it is our richly patterned making sense of the situation. It binds us deeply with the world and opens up fresh vistas.

It's also a feeling of blended surprise and recognition. Our journey began with our being given some puzzlement or wonder. Also, in our coming to know, we have trusted ourselves to a tiny tacit sense of where we are going, of the yet-to-be-known. We can also have had a sense we are getting closer to it. Our partially successful, subsidiarily anticipative indwelling of the clues has been responsible for this. This guiding sense isn't something we could have put in words. In the moment of epiphany, we feel recognition because we anticipated the pattern; we feel surprise because it is transformatively more than we expected.

We experience joy and delight. The knowledge-as-information orientation contains no place for delight and excitement. Yet these responses should be counted as epistemically significant. Delight and excitement are felt body responses on which we rely to guide us toward a discovery. They also signal that insight has been graciously given to us.

We feel a sense of grace. An epiphany, in the moment, feels very much like a gracious gift from outside us, no matter how much effort we have invested. And that would be correct. All the love, pledge, and sacrifice we have given do not merit the gift we receive, even though it invites it. They have not determined the outcome. Nor do the particulars of our puzzlement entirely account for their transformation into subsidiaries. The breakthrough insight is so lavish, profound, and superior that we easily see we could not have forced it, reasoned to it, or reached it on our own without gracious help from beyond us. Reality itself has met us and gifted itself to us.

We feel a sense of grace. But this is no burden. It's not as if we say, glumly, I didn't deserve this. Remember that epiphany is accompanied by a feeling of delight and joy. What we feel is happy thankfulness. To be glum, to beat ourselves up about not deserving something, is to be acting out merit, not grace.

And we need to sustain this sense of grace. To let ourselves forget that we did not deserve the insight, to become complacent and proud in it, is to step away from savvy knowing practice and readiness for further knowing ventures. It is a kind of reversion to the power dynamic of the knowledge-as-information stance. It is to become less mature in love, and less qualified to invite the real. And it is to disrespect, to depersonalize, to objectify the world, bending it to our own purposes and vanity. It is to hurt, rather than heal, the world. We want to sustain this sense of grace into our ongoing commitment to what we have found. To do this is to retain wonder in ordinary knowing. It is to insist that knowing be rooted, not in power, but in love.

Embedded in the epiphany is a shift from active to passive, from giving to receiving. It feels like a shift from knowing to being known. We invested much in finding; we find that we have been found. We are the one or ones who have been looked for. This goes with the fact noted before that the pattern gives transformative meaning to the clues. But our sense is that reality has taken it upon itself to break in generously and make sense of our world.

Our sense, in the moment of insight, is of having contacted a reality that is three-dimensionally bigger than what we had had in mind hitherto. It is bigger than a simple answer to our question; it reshapes our question—or questions us. Even as we experience understanding, we sense farther vistas and depths. We sense that our insight comes on its terms, not ours. For all that we feel more intimately, profoundly connected with the known. Our experiences of knowing as insight in turn modify our metaphysical outlook: reality becomes bigger, dynamic, close, generous, transformatively invested in us.

Insight as encounter

Because of this shift and how it feels we experience epiphany as a moment of *encounter*. In the famous phrase of philosopher Martin Buber, it is an I-You encounter. It is not a subjective, private experience. Rather, we stand in a relation in which we give ourselves and receive another. In this moment we connect with reality in a mutual, personal giving. We are indwelling it and it is indwelling us. It is a moment of communion in which we are intimate with the object of our quest. Our love invited the real; the real comes into our love and flourishes there. The relationship we have with it is invested, compassionate, connected. It's not a mercenary help-yourself. We didn't invite it by exhibiting that attitude. Now it stands before us in our delight and wonder. Now it stands before us in mutual consent. We may not take it for granted.

Encounter is why it makes sense to see knowing as cultivating an interpersonal relationship between knower and known. It shows why an approach of inviting the real makes sense. For this is how reality comes. Our experience of knowing as encounter, in turn, should reshape our sense of reality. Reality is not passive, indifferent, collectible information tidbits. It is dynamic, generous, always surprisingly new. It responds to overtures of love. We hold a special place in its regard: we could say it wants to be known by us.

In the first chapter we identified the normative dimension of reality and our relationship to it, as well as the generous gifting character of the real. We reprise it here. Having come to understand and embrace SFI, we have a better grasp of this way of seeing reality.

Seeing knowing as encounter shows again how it is that successful knowings themselves mature us in love as persons and as knowers. Moments of epiphany open us up and out to giving ourselves more and more in love. This is because they affect the fourth dimension of our humanness, coming into our Void—the gracious inbreaking deliverance, the possibility of new being—the Holy.

Contact with reality and "IFMs"

The feeling of epiphany is one of excitement. Our excitement affirms that we have, in this integration, made contact with reality. How do we know we have made contact with reality? What is it about the integration that gives us this sense? Simply, it is the depth and richness of it. It is rich in regard to what went before—retrospectively; and it is rich in regard to the future—prospectively. It is rich retrospectively in that it not only makes sense of what we were puzzled about, it makes sense of much more than it had yet occurred to us to be puzzled about. And it is less like it answers our question and more like it reshapes the question. It changes our reality more than fitting into it. Rather than it fitting into our sense of what makes sense, it fits us into its sense of what makes sense. It makes such surprisingly recognizable sense that we find ourselves in a new world—its world, on its turf—from which it would be unwelcome and probably impossible to go back. We can't unlearn to read, for example. Once we learn to read we are forever readers.

A successful integration is rich prospectively, also. We know we have made contact with reality because we get a sense of wonderful future possibilities that we cannot name. These are "indeterminate future manifestations"—IFMs. A good integrative pattern is fraught with promise. It promises the unfolding of dimensions and horizons and discoveries that we haven't begun to imagine. It promises vistas of further yet-to-be-knowns. We have indwelt the subsidiaries that support this integrative pattern. We have extended our felt body sense to incorporate them. Now we are again orienting toward fertile regions beyond where we are. IFMs become the clues of our further journey. IFMs and excitement go hand-in-hand.

The possibilities and prospects can be endless. But this in no way means they are random. They have a significant character—it is the character of the real that we are coming to know. We are coming to rely on that character even as we appreciate its surprising three-dimensionality. Reality is inexhaustive and surprising and dynamic in its self-revealing, but it isn't random, and it isn't whatever we arbitrarily want it to be. Knowing never stops requiring our submission to and respect for the real.

Epiphany may end one journey and begin another. Or better: it transmutes the one journey into another. We are always on a knowing venture. It isn't that it feels futile or disheartening—as if we never reach the end of our journey. It feels like a never-ending joyous adventure. We have embarked on an unfolding relationship of knower to known. We can give ourselves to it in trust and confidence, anticipating its abundant reward. Knowing ventures require and reward trusting reality to give good gifts.

Pledge-based verification

If we know we have made contact with reality because of unspecifiable retrospective and prospective richness, because of profound transformation of our venture, and because of IFMs, then justifying our conviction about reality is going to have to be more informal than formal. Our sense of contact is itself something we can't fully put in words. At first this sense is all we have. We often do go on to develop formal testing and verification of our initial insight. But it is important to see the most formal testing and critical verification—just like the initial insight—requires, in similar measure, our informal, personal commitment to affirm its validity and confirm the original insight. Our informal sense of the rightness of our conviction always roots and justifies our formal confirmation.

We never replace the loving-in-order-to-know orientation or revert to a knowledge-as-information model. Truth isn't a bare collection of obvious facts. It is a profession of allegiance—a highly sophisticated, pledge-like human act. Proof doesn't begin a journey, and it doesn't end it either. Rather, responsible pledge figures in to the journey accompanying the vast range of subsidiary clues on which we rely. Insight and verification expand our artful subsidiary grasp of things; they don't eliminate it.

Moving on from epiphany

Epiphany, the moment of insight, involves all these great feelings. But we don't linger indefinitely in that moment, in the face-to-face gaze of encounter. Yes, the moment of insight we know to be an experience of grace. We need to retain that sense of grace. But such a gracious self-disclosure of the real calls us freely, joyously, to give ourselves again in pledged response or personal responsibility of faithfulness to this newly disclosed and disclosing reality. Love and faithfulness go together. We submit freely to this fresh reality, binding ourselves to our further understanding and its further disclosure, binding ourselves to its integrity. In the wake of epiphany, we soon plunge into what can be arduous labor to work our fresh insight out into our lives, to reorient our lives to its reality, to bring others into this new reality.

However, the aura of the encounter stays with us. The encounter has transformed us—the topic of the next chapter. Also, we can revisit the wonder of the encounter. Just as we revisit Middle Earth every time we open Tolkien's *Lord of the Rings*, so we can attend afresh to our moment of epiphany. It can be a moment to soak afresh in the wonder, to re-center, to celebrate our relationship with the real. This is a good thing to be intentional about doing, so that the aura of graced epiphany continues to surround our ongoing knowing venture. It keeps our knowing venture balanced on the keel of love.

The miracle and dynamism of the encounter remains permanently ensconced in the wonder-full, two-level, subsidiary-focal structure of all sustained knowing. As we grow in artful awareness of that subsidiary dimension, we become even better at knowing and at embracing the real.

Epiphanies in our knowing ventures

In our knowing ventures any sort of breakthrough, any Eureka moment, qualifies as this moment of encounter. For an artist or designer, it is the moment of *inspiration*. It's telling that we call it that: the word's Latin origins suggest the breathed-in influence of a god. In a business or ministry team it may be a fresh thought birthed in a focus group or brainstorming session that the group quickly senses is on the right track. In a classroom or in study it is the student's or class's light-bulb experience. In athletics it is the moment our body gets it and we reconnect to our body. In self-discovery it is the moment of self-realization. In relationship with God it is the redemptive encounter.

Identifying these critical moments of encounter as central to knowing is key to reorienting our epistemic orientation to one of love, and our knowing venture to one of joyous, healing, productivity. They also shape our recharacterization of and appreciation for reality. We love in order to know. We find ourselves embraced in the depths of an other.

Exercises for your knowing venture

1. In your knowing venture, identify your moments of insight. As you describe them identify the shift that is the moment of integration. In what ways does your experience of it fit with what has been described here? Specifically:

   a. The rightness of your discovery.

   b. Surprise.

   c. Recognition.

2. What additional features do you experience?

   a. Joy and delight.

   b. A sense of grace.

   c. A sense of reality's generous gift.

   d. A shift from active to passive.

   e. Finding and being found, knowing and being known.

   f. I-You encounter.

   g. Connectedness with situation, authoritative guidance, and body sense.

   h. The fourth dimension of humanness—the Holy.

   i. Further maturation into self-giving love.

   j. Greater wisdom regarding knowing.

   k. A sense of having made contact with reality.

   l. Excitement at future prospects—IFMs.

   m. A reshaping of your understanding of your knowing venture.

3. How can you and your team appropriately celebrate your moment of insight? How may you in the future return to the wonder of this moment and draw strength and reorientation from it?

4. What does it look like now for you and your team to move on from this moment of insight?

5. What will be involved in verification of your fresh insight? In what ways is it evident that such verification is itself pledge-based?

6. In what ways must you work out this integration into your life?

7. Identify the features of knowing that remain in your sustained commitment to the reality you have discovered—specifically, love, pledge, faithfulness, and subsidiary-focal awareness.

CHAPTER 6

Transformation

I NSIGHT ISN'T INFORMATIONAL; IT is transformational. It is a knowing event. A change transpires. Understanding this distinction makes a big difference to all our knowing ventures. The moment of insight transforms the knower, the known, and the knowing. Obviously this shapes how we go forward from epiphany. Carrying out our knowing ventures with a view to transformation makes us better at them.

A transformed knower

The moment of epiphany transforms the knower. Humanness, we saw earlier, consists of more than the two dimensions of a self coping with a situation. The Void—being faced with the possibility of non-being—is a third, unavoidable, dimension of humanness. Embracing the Void also fuels our longing to know. Out of our need, our sense of what we do not yet understand, we reach forward to embrace the knowing venture. We identified the fourth dimension of humanness, also, when we talked about becoming the self that responds to and gives love. The Holy is the gracious possibility of new being. It also suggests that this is an interpersonal event.

In the moment of epiphany we are undergoing the breaking in of a new way of being. We sense it as a gracious deliverance. Every moment of insight is growing the fourth dimension of our humanness. We talked before about how maturity in love develops in our lives as we are persons in communion—as we know ourselves in the noticing regard of others. Since all knowing events are relational and the knower is in some way being known, all knowing events contribute to this maturation. We mature to be selves who give themselves in love, able to love in order to know. In this way, knowing transforms the knower, and makes the knower better at knowing ventures.

Epiphany is encounter, the encounter of I with You. Martin Buber also says that through encounters such as discovery and artistic creation, the knower grows to become "the I of I-You." The I of I-You is a fully-personed I, readied to respond to the known in interpersoned relationship. We bring this maturity into all our future knowing. We bring the wonder and love that invites and unlocks the real, even in the seemingly impersonal and indifferent situations.

Another way the knower is transformed in the knowing event has to do with the way we have come to indwell the subsidiaries. In coming to know we are trying to indwell subsidiaries from our body, from the normative directions of authoritative guides, and from the situation that puzzles us. Before the aha! moment, all three dimensions can have felt opaque and meaningless—even our own bodies. After the moment of insight, when we succeed in indwelling these subsidiarily, directions have melded with our felt body sense, and made sense of the situation. This is like acquiring a skill; it *is* acquiring a skill. We bodily live the directions, now, and we view the world from this new outlook. We have expanded our capacity and savvy. We have advanced our wisdom. And we can advance in our virtuosity.

Also, our felt body sense expands to include all that is subsidiary in our knowing. This includes our language and cultural traditions, our worldview, special interpretative grids and directions and strategies we have applied in our knowing venture, and skilled use of tools. In these ways, the knower is transformed in the knowing event.

Here is another way that insight changes the knower, one mentioned in the last chapter. A profound discovery doesn't so much answer our questions as reshape our questions. It reshapes the way we see the world and the inquiry we pursue from that point on. A pilgrimage of knowing can be a journey of course corrections. We may have begun facing west, so to speak; gradually we find ourselves facing another direction, moving toward an endpoint that we could in no way have imagined at the outset. So insights recalibrate our coordinates as we pursue our knowing venture. Each fresh perspective is one that accords more harmoniously with the world. The knower has been transformed to dwell in deeper communion with the yet-to-be-known.

Along with these changes, the knower grows confident in knowing. Knowing, after all, is itself a skill. But since it is also growing a relationship with the world, we grow the capacity to trust ourselves and the world in our knowing ventures. Paralyzing anxiety subsides as anticipation takes on a more adventurous aspect.

Finally, the transformed knower becomes a transformer. People who have insights and now go joyously looking for them inspire others to engage the world in this way. We can tantalize others to seek to become the I of I-You encounter. This is the implicit passion of any good teacher. After all, any interpersonal relationship is itself an act of knowing. It is obviously an interpersonal act of knowing. So in that relationship, as in any knowing venture, we invite the real. The knower's transformation, confidence, love, and pledge, winsomely woos others to the posture of loving in order to know. This is something we can be intentional about so as to grow as a team in our knowing venture.

Reality transformed

The knowing event transforms the known also. In the moment of insight, the knower has finally come to a pattern of meaning that makes sense of the situation. This is a disclosure of the real, and it invites the further disclosure of the real. It's as if reality breathes a sigh of relief because now it has been heard and has been given a voice. Learning how to post on a trotting horse is a good example of this. Reality can now speak truthfully. It can give in a way that accords naturally with its character. It can grow to be more itself than perhaps has been possible before. It can grow to be better. This is what "knowing for shalom" means: good, healthy, knowing practice ought to foster healing in the known as it does in the knower.

In our moment of insight lies a kind of betrothal to the real. The real now can trust our ongoing, responsible, covenant faithfulness to it. We betroth ourselves to stewarding it with integrity, faithful to its dignity and cultivation. In such covenanted space, the real may freely grow more fully into itself.

The world becomes, in a moment of insight, a world in which such a thing can be true and can come to be. It has a deeper rationality. It is a world in which we can see that other things will be reasonable—and some formerly reasonable things no longer so. This contributes to the IFMs we experience when we make contact with reality.

Insight heightens our sense that reality itself is gift, just as is any successful insight. It heightens our sense of wonder (not doubt or fear) that real things might not be there, and might not be the way they are. That they are has to do with their being promised and bestowed. As we said before, this is a Christian theological vision. The idea of reality as gift is uniquely at home in the Christian vision. But seeing reality this way makes anybody better at knowing ventures.

Transformed knowing

So epiphany transforms the knower, and it transforms the known. Finally, it transforms knowing. Each moment of insight makes us better at the art of knowing and at all our knowing ventures.

It improves our epistemology, if we let it. Insight itself redraws our understanding of what it is to know. If we attend to it, as we are in this little book, epiphany confirms that we love in order to know. Knowing—the relationship between knower and known—is an interpersonal one. In the moment of insight we are also blessed to glimpse the relational dynamism of engaging the real. We may respond by becoming better lovers.

Transformation in our knowing ventures

In college it is a wonderful thing when students wake up to the joy of learning, to experience insight, to respond with responsible covenantal engagement—to come alive as knowers. For them, reality transforms as they transform as knowers. Commencement becomes, quite truly, a beginning worth celebrating. Education is not information impersonally collected and regurgitated; it is transformative re-formation as knowers covenanted joyously to engage the world in a stewardly way.

Business, research, and design involve teams of people who are shaped by and shape the world and society through their knowing ventures. Where breakthroughs are deemed encounters and ventures are balanced on the keel of covenant love and faithfulness, not only will the world be blessed, but knowing will be more effective. Employees will be happier and more productive, because they will be wholly human.

Artists, in artistic encounter, grow to trust reality and voice it to the rest of us. Works of art that are encounters repeatedly become encounters for the viewers. Artists mature in the process, as is evident to any attentive patron. Culture is transformatively enriched and can be healed. Art is commonly employed in therapy—and no wonder.

Care-givers, community-servers, ministry teams, are transformed, as are the subjects of their mission, in the moments when they are blessed with profound insight into the specific shape of their mission. They light on an effective strategy; then they find that strategy shapes them and the targeted community. They come to see the whole thing in a transformatively different way, and they joyously bind themselves to bringing it to be.

Where relationship with God is the knowing venture in view, of course redemptive encounter means transformation. You cannot be known by God without being different and being forever in joyously unfolding relationship with him.

Individual athletes can experience a kind of body breakthrough or mental breakthrough that qualitatively raises the level of their performance. Athletic teams can find a way of teaming that transforms the output of all together.

In any sort of knowing venture, then, insight proves transformational.

Exercises for your knowing venture

1. Describe how insight in your knowing venture has transformed or is transforming you and your team. Specifically:

   a. Is it maturing you as knowers and as a team?

   b. How have normative maxims and the meaningfulness of the situation melded with your felt body sense? How is this expanding your skills, your capacity, your savvy, and your virtuosity?

   c. How has your insight drawn on and given fresh significance to your language, traditions, life history, and theoretical frameworks? How has it called them into question?

   d. Has your integrative insight reshaped your original questions? What are your new questions?

   e. How has this epiphany given you a fresh perspective on the world and on your knowing venture? In what way has it recalibrated your coordinates?

   f. Describe any change you notice in your confidence as a knower, your readiness to trust yourself and the world in future knowing ventures?

   g. Ask your coworkers and friends whether they notice your transformation, and whether they see it drawing others to engage the world transformatively.

2. In what ways has your insight transformed the world, and the very thing you were seeking? Specifically:

   a. What about the situation seems to have healed, or attained peace and wellbeing as result of new freedom to be itself?

---

b. How does reality now display a deeper rationality?

c. How has reality revealed itself afresh as gift?

3. In what ways does your experience attaining a moment of epiphany in your knowing venture reshape your understanding of how knowing works? How is this experience reshaping your underlying epistemology?

CHAPTER 7

Dance

T HE KNOWING VENTURE IS a pilgrimage together, inaugurated in love, shaped by pledge, advanced through invitation, driven through indwelling, climaxing in the encounter of insight that transforms knower and known. And now we add that the knowing venture is carried forward in the dynamic of dance, and culminates in communion.

How we designate our knowing venture—where it begins and what it concerns—can vary. We can target something specific and single, such as learning the Pythagorean Theorem, or we can designate the venture as something much larger, such as mastery and expertise in mathematical discovery. Actually, we can see our whole lives as one big knowing venture. Larger knowing ventures contain multiple smaller ones. Smaller ventures open out into larger ones.

Whether we see our venture as a specific one having a single goal, or a larger one composed of multiple stages, the dynamic of our ongoing involvement in it can be seen as a dance. Dance characterizes the unfolding venture as it moves toward insight, and it also typifies the ongoing relationship once insight has occurred. So it helps our venture to attend to this dynamic.

What makes a dance a dance?

We can imagine a couple swing dancing, or a group dance such as a Serbian dance. Each member of the dance gives, and then receives, to-and-fro, in moving relationship. There is overture, and then there is response. Each partner gives, and then each receives. Overture and response unfolds through time. It unfolds in the dance, as it has unfolded as the couple has learned the dance together.

You could say that at any particular moment, one individual is off balance. Each takes a turn, in turn, leaning in trust toward the other. But between them in the relationship, they sustain dynamically an ongoing, overall balance. This is just the dance. The dance can be artful and beautiful. And the goal is itself ongoing relational communion, in the dance, and in blessing the world.

Partners in knowing

A dancelike dynamic is implicit in loving in order to know. It helps to identify and start to sense and work with this dynamic in our knowing. Knowing can be seen as the dance of knower with known. The motif of dance helps us grow steady confidence in the give and take of knowing, and mutual trust in our relationship with the known. It makes us better knowers because we have the feel of it.

Any knowing venture is just an unfolding relationship between knower(s) and yet-to-be-known. Dance is relationship unfolding in a back-and-forth, gently, artfully, healthfully. It injects beauty into the relationship. It is knower and known working together, not at cross-purposes. It treats both partners with respect and trust. Effective knowing takes knower and known relating in artful overture and response.

Identifying this dynamic helps us overcome the temptation to expect that knowing is linear, passive, information collecting—one-way, over and done. It also helps overcome the idea that the knower entirely creates and determines whatever is "known," and is utterly responsible for it. In an epistemology of loving-in-order-to-know, we can expect that we should find that a mutually self-giving gesture such as dance characterizes our ventures.

Knowing: personal relationship and appropriate etiquette

Viewing knowing as dance underscores that knowing is a relationship that is person-like. Even if the thing to be known isn't a person, it makes us better knowers to accord it the respect, dignity, humility, and so on, that interpersonal relationship requires. And even if two persons aren't dancing, dance is the dynamic of interpersonal relationship. We move to and fro in conversations, in growing understanding, in growing solidarity and mutual trust. This is how relationship unfolds. In our knowing venture, we are in relationship with the yet-to-be-known.

Dance as gift

The dynamic of dance is the dynamic of gift. It is the dynamic of mutual self-giving, and thus of love. So there is something ceremonial about it, a polite request: "Here I am" and "will you please?" It hopes for gracious consent. It presumes and usurps nothing. This ceremonial overture and consent is something only persons can do. It renders it gift.

These are the telltale normative features of knowing and of reality that we have noted again and again. Our pledge and reality's consent constitute knowing. Also, that knowing involves mutual gift means the entire venture is grace-based. Our investment is gracious, as is its result.

Keeping this very human, relational, ceremonial dimension in mind keeps our knowing balanced on the keel of love. We honor and invite a person-like reality through our gentle, pledge-like overture: "This is for you; will you please?" "May I have this dance?"

All this underscores the idea of etiquette. Our knowing ventures can be rendered more effective, we have seen, by identifying, and practicing with intentionality, the pledge that constitutes a venture, and the etiquette appropriate to persons.

Knowing: overture and response

The dynamic of knowing is overture and response. In our knowing ventures, we should notice that we take a step, make an overture, and then wait for response. In light of the response we take another step, and then look for further response. A waltz is liable to move a couple around the entire dance floor. So our journey, and our relationship, in its overture and response, moves us together in surprising though recognizable directions.

Overture and response, of course, involves mutuality and reciprocity. Each is "for" the other, each gesture in hope of response. The knower, actively, responsibly loves and invests. The knower also submits to reality. Without this mutual reciprocity, there is no dancing with the real.

In all our knowing ventures we can identify the to-and-fro of knower and known. Attending to this helps us make the most of the dynamic. It helps us cultivate our sense of when to initiate and when to wait and receive. It helps us treat with patient, humble respect the times reality gives as well as the times it resists. Plus, our specific knowing venture very well has a distinctive dance of its own. How we woo one sort of reality ought to be different from how we woo another.

Asymmetry

Overture and response are asymmetric. First one partner acts while the other receives, then the other acts while the first receives. Gift, as we said before, in order to be gift, cannot be a tit-for-tat exchange. That is what we call a trade, not a gift. Asymmetry is the dynamic that keeps gift, gift. A dance requires asymmetry to move forward. Each move is a gesture of hope—in hope of gracious response. Each partner has to be okay being off balance for a time, and waiting for and trusting the upcoming move of the partner.

This is the dynamic of the knowing venture, also. We bind ourselves in pledge and discipline to the inquiry; but we wait in hope for insight. We may not presume. What comes is often not exactly what we anticipated, and we find that is perhaps better. We move forward again, taking a risk that our effort will be rewarded, and waiting to see if it is. Just as we might gently tame a wild animal or coax a child to join in a game, in knowing we see that the overtures and responses of knower and known are asymmetric: in turn, and ever the gestures of grace.

Rhythm

In dance the reciprocal overture and response is rhythmic. It isn't random or haphazard. It involves growing a subsidiary, felt body sense and skill. And once we have got the rhythm, peace and well-being come to reign as we can embrace the ongoing risk of the dance with expert awareness and steady delight. Similarly, knowers mature in the skill of knowing, a skill that involves a body sense, one that is better for being cultivated as rhythmical—or at least anticipated.

In our questioning, for example, we can be both systematic and gracious. We ask and then we listen. We map out a course of inquiry, holding to it openly enough, and creatively, to revise it in light of surprising outcomes. We give ourselves to a project and we reap the results with grace, allowing it to shape us and our further engagement of reality. We can give ourselves with intentionality to this dynamic in a rhythmic way. This rhythm contributes to the overall health of our lives and our productivity as knowers.

Artistry

Rhythmical dance can grow to be artful. There are capable dancers, and then there are artful, virtuoso dancers. We can grow artistry in our knowing ventures. And when we are able, we want to apprentice ourselves to master knowers who exhibit such artistry. Artistry involves beauty. Our knowing venture can come to exhibit beauty, and in the process grow in effectiveness. Of course, such artistry is also wisdom.

Often knowing ventures are not as blissful as all this sounds. They're not infused with play so much as desperation. Even so, desperate and quick overtures and responses drive the venture forward. Perhaps this is more like a *paso doble* than a waltz. Nevertheless, all the features described here pertain to those desperate situations. In desperate situations, we desperately trust ourselves to the dynamic of dance. Indwelling, skill, and artistry are all the more evident. If we don't have them or trust them, the venture aborts.

An obvious example of this is the pressure at the end of a college semester. Another is the time just prior to a deadline. The dance can become furious! But it can remain a dance for those skilled in inviting the real in pledged, rhythmic reciprocity. We find that the disciplines of the dance developed in the more waltz-like earlier stages of our venture can actually, under pressure, enable a substantial increase in output.

But the image of dance reminds us that we may not, under pressure, break the rules. We may not plagiarize; we may not fabricate data. To dishonor the truth is to dishonor reality. It is to break the dance and to cripple ourselves as knowers.

Relational health, balancing relatedness and individuality

The metaphor of dance also suggests a healthy relationship. What makes a relationship healthy is a balance of relatedness and particular individuality. You don't lose the relationship to the individuality, and you don't lose the individuality in the relationship. Relatedness and particularity should not be adversarial opposites. It's not that we work out a compromise somewhere in between, so that the partners are neither totally related nor totally individual. Rather, what we are looking to grow is a relationship that makes each particular individual more themselves, and a particularity that makes the relationship stronger.

This is relational health. Psychologists call it differentiation, and underscore that it is a process. To say it is a process is to say that it unfolds; we could say it unfolds and is sustained like a dance.

Dance models this harmony of relatedness and individual particularity. It is in healthy relationship that a particular person or thing is given space and regard so as to grow to be more itself, to thrive and to bless the world. We saw just this dynamic when we talked about persons maturing in love in the regard of and communion with other persons. To give space and regard is a gesture of hospitality. The host courteously welcomes the stranger in his or her home space. To say, "Welcome!" is a very personable, highly sophisticated "let there be." Creating a hospitable space confers liberty along with dignity—liberty for the yet-to-be-known to make itself known truly. It takes welcome and liberty to avoid a pressure that compels a skewed disclosure or issues in no response at all.

Our knowing ventures should relate us and the yet-to-be-known in such a way that neither is lost in the relationship, but rather each becomes more itself. Neither knower nor known should have to sacrifice their integrity. Both should move toward greater wholeness.

Of course, there are times when a knower may wonder whether this is happening. Consider, for example, a PhD candidate buried in the research for a dissertation. But finalized degrees ought to represent the maturation of knowers. A knower embroiled in a dissertation must work to hold onto her or himself in the process, in hope of future vindication.

On the part of the known, there is much at stake in the probing knower getting it right. A machine or a plant can suffer and even be broken by human attempts to figure it out. But this just underscores the need for those endeavoring to understand to move forward with gentleness and respect.

Warring opposites or ultimate peace?

Life is often difficult and our best efforts are thwarted. We often mess things up ourselves. But it is really important to believe that the way things are, when all is said and done, is not a state of chaos and warring, but rather a state of peace and well-being and beauty. Reality is bountiful gift, not violent, indifferent, or meaningless. It makes a difference what you think "normal" is, and what you can hope to develop in your living and knowing. It makes a difference to believe that relatedness and individuality can be balanced in the rhythmical dynamic of dance, that the norm is not either a tense compromise or the one absorbing the other. It makes a difference to think of relatedness and individuality as each enhancing the other. It makes a difference to believe that this is possible, to envision beauty, peace, and well-being. This hope makes a real, palpable difference to our own health, to the health of our knowing venture, and to the health of the world.

This view of reality is, once again, uniquely a Christian vision—a vision that Christianity alone says is true of the world. In the Christian understanding of reality, the most real thing is the Holy Trinity: three Persons bound in a joyous dance in which each becomes more himself, and creation is the overflow of their exuberance. Just about any other vision of the world struggles to balance warring opposites. The Christian vision is at its heart about hospitably, graciously welcoming the other to be with and to be within.

But the point here is that to see the knowing venture as a dance means that we are better at knowing if we aspire to its picture of relational health between knower and known. It makes sense to aspire to it, if we think that reality itself has this dynamic.

The dancelike interplay
of subsidiary and focal awareness

We can apply the dance dynamic when thinking of knower and known in our unfolding knowing adventure. But we can also see it operate in other places in our knowing itself. It describes the lively interplay between subsidiary and focal in SFI. We want to attend from the subsidiaries in a way that makes the focal appear and stand out. But we want to attend to the focus in a way that treats the subsidiary, even as subsidiary, with integrity. Focal and subsidiary should be seen to be linked in a dynamic of mutual reciprocity. Each makes the other what it is, in relationship. We grow as knowers as we develop a dancing relationship between them. We can develop a dancing duality of awareness. In fact, this is just what this *Little Manual* has begun, by calling attention to the existence of subsidiary awareness and its necessary partnership in all knowing. To grow in intentional and skilled awareness of the subsidiaries in the focus of a performance is to develop virtuosity. In our knowing ventures, we can rhythmically intersperse the times we go to the golf course (focal) with the times we return to the driving range (subsidiaries temporarily analyzed).

Dancing among the clues

We can also apply the dance metaphor to the way we spiral, in our coming to know, from one sector of clues to another and back again. In our knowing we put together clues from our felt body sense, from the normative maxims of authoritative guides, and from the situation. We can see the process as situating ourselves first in one sector to view the others, and then in another, and then in the third. We navigate our way toward an intersection of the three. We indwell the guidance we receive, seeking to align our felt body sense to it, and seeing how it makes sense of the world. We need the world to bring three-dimensionality to the guidance, the way roads make a map three-dimensional. We grow our felt body sense as we bring both within us in our felt sense. Each sector helps shed light on the others, and more each time around.

So for example: a good college course involves all three sectors, as does good learning. Lectures, directions, and expert hands-on guidance and texts are normative. The students (and the class as a whole) give themselves in pledge and submission. Together, professor and class explore the subject and the situation, connecting the words with the world. This makes sense of the words and evokes the world. It helps students see what is there, and it brings the world to be more itself. The course interweaves these three dimensions. And it does so, by the way, riding the dancing dynamic of interpersonal relationship of expert and apprentice.

Communion with the real
—the dancelike goal of knowing ventures

Knowing involves a dancing dynamic of rhythmic reciprocity. This is true when you are on the way to knowing, and it is still true once you have achieved insight. To know in fullness is to sustain a rhythmic reciprocity in relationship with the known, in focal and subsidiary awareness, and in the mutual interpenetration of norms, situation, and felt body sense. All the maturation of our love is fulfilled in ongoing, covenantal communion with reality. The knowing venture does not end in stagnation. It "ends" in the sense that it is consummated, not in the sense that it is over. The goal of our knowing venture is achieved in well-being and peace in ongoing relationship of knower and known. The goal of knowing is not complete information; it is communion.

If we think that knowledge is so much information to amass, then the goal of knowing is comprehensive information. We surmise that this isn't possible, and so we can feel that we are condemned, like Sisyphus, to the journey. However, an epistemology of love transforms our outlook. The joy is truly in the journey, because the attainable goal is ongoing, peaceable communion. This is not to settle for second best as a vision of knowing. It is to shift to embrace a transformative alternative, a covenantally relational vision. And we can anticipate with joy that relational communion, once achieved, is only the beginning of a never-ending adventure of mutual discovery and delight.

Reality is not such that we can exhaust it. Reality is continuously dynamic, ever-new gift. It harbors mystery and surprise, always. But we and it are meant to trust each other and thrive in that trust. This is the joy of communion.

And while life and knowing is often thwarted and broken and difficult, we still have a choice how to view it as we set about knowing. Choosing dancing toward communion invites the real. It makes us better knowers even as it makes us better lovers.

Dancing ventures of knowing

Bringing the vision of dance into our understanding of knowing ventures deepens our grasp of all that we have said so far about knowing. It amplifies it by displaying, and helping us feel and trust, the beauty of loving in order to know. It also takes the discussion further: it helps us see how we proceed in our venture, beyond the transformative moment of encounter, into sustained relationship with the real. It indicates something simple but profound both about the goal of our venture and of our hope for the world.

Exercises for your knowing venture

1. At this point in your knowing venture, how are you designating your venture? Have you found that it includes additional specific ventures? Have you found that it is embedded in a larger venture? If so, identify these.

2. Choose an example of dancing, or tell an experience of it, that you can have in mind as you discuss this chapter. Identify some notable features of the dynamic.

3. In what ways does your knowing venture exhibit a dancelike dynamic of overture and response? Specifically:

    a. Between knower and known.

    b. Between normative, bodily, and situational subsidiaries.

    c. Between subsidiary and focal awareness.

    d. Between team members.

    e. When has the dance been measured and when has it been frantic?

---

4. How does this idea of dance bring to greater light the loving-in-order-to-know approach in your venture?

5. How can you and your team be more intentional in moving with the dancelike dynamic of knowing? For example, what would it look like to develop an artful rhythm in your engagement with reality?

6. Suggest some ways in which moving intentionally with the dancelike dynamic of knowing will have positive results for your venture.

7. Identify the relationality and particularity in your venture's relationship between knower and known. Assess the relational health of this balance. What are some things you are doing well? What are some things that need work? What are some changes you could make to this end?

8. Consider your sense of the ultimate way things are. Is yours a vision of peace or a vision of strife? What rationale supports your outlook? Are you able to buy the idea that peace is the larger vision? Why or why not? How does your ultimate vision impact the way you engage your knowing venture?

9. How does it shape your outlook in your knowing venture to conceive the goal to be ongoing relational communion or friendship with what you hope to discover? To the extent that you have already achieved insight, in what ways do you see communion (as opposed to conquest or comprehensive information) occurring?

10. How does the motif of dance aid you as you cultivate ongoing relationship with what you have discovered?

CHAPTER 8

Shalom

HERE AT THE END of the *Little Manual,* and also possibly of your knowing venture, we consider the end of knowing. But just as a look at the outset of the knowing venture—love—highlighted the stark contrast of its orientation to an orientation of knowledge as information, so a look at the end of the venture highlights the contrast. A knowledge-as-information approach is about results. Performance. Control. Outcomes. Success. Power. Wealth. Consumption. The loving-in-order-to-know approach of this *Little Manual* is about results of a noticeably different sort. If we love in order to know, we know for shalom. Resolution. Healing. Relationship. Joy. Peace.—*And* better outcomes.

The Magi of Epiphany returned home from their pilgrimage, rejoicing in the insight of encounter, of being known, by the Lord of all. They were made new, as was their world. And more than any other pilgrimage we can think of, the promise of this one was peace. We continue to live in that promise, looking for its full fruition.

And this vision of shalom is, if only in a small way, actualized in our knowing. We may know for shalom. With every knowing venture we may invite it and contribute to it.

Resolution

How is it that we know for shalom? Accompanying the moment of insight there is a relief and resolution that comes as we figure something out. The "aha!" of insight includes the "ah" of release. A tension is resolved, bringing peace. That tension includes the fact that we have been sensing something but not yet knowing what it was we were sensing. When reality self-discloses, even as it surprises us in the way it does it, it nevertheless accords peaceably with our anticipations.

We often say that we have connected the dots, made sense of something. We say that with a smile, because it just feels good. We feel that we have put more things together. That is a tiny bit of shalom.

The fresh pattern of SFI is a transformatively deeper vision that makes peace among apparently warring opposites. Prior to an integration, the particulars of our concern may actually have appeared to be contradictory. The integration supplies a larger context in which they are not just balanced or made to compromise, but rather, resolved. And we are brought into harmony with the world. A fresh integrative pattern melds together ourselves and the things that we didn't understand. We find that we have been caught up into a larger pattern, a larger vision, a reality larger and grander than we had hitherto realized.

A fresh integration redraws reality to help its pieces work together. It solves problems. Good knowing can unleash reality itself to be more itself.

None of this is the mere absence of conflict. It is creative resolution. It is the profoundly positive peace of something grander.

Healing

Resolution leads to healing and wholeness. Healing and wholeness are of a piece with shalom. Earlier we saw how being known by the other brings personal maturation in love, and how every knowing event contributes in a small way to that. We saw how for most of us our journey to maturation must also be a path of healing, in which we cry out in hope from the Void and look for the gracious inbreaking deliverance of the Holy. We've talked about how knowing transforms us, the knower. We've seen how it involves encounter, and thus the sense of composed confidence that comes with personal relationship. All this is shalom.

Knowing also heals the known—that is, it should do so. Just as understanding our plants and bushes and trees leads to their health, knowing blesses reality with healing. A doctor's correct assessment of an ear infection prompts its healing. A coach's diagnosis of a defective batting swing leads to a stronger, faster, easier-on-the-body effort.

A loving-to-know approach heals knowing itself. That is epistemology for shalom. We'll return to this presently.

Communion

And the goal of knowing is communion. This is an ongoing, dynamic, joyous, fruitful, friendship—not a one-sided power domination, over with a triumph of information collection. Communion contrasts to power in affording a lively, joyous, fruitful, peace. In contrast to the mastery of nature that characterized the centuries of modernity, knowers' goal with the known is relationship, not conquest. This is a vision that accords more responsibly with our understanding of the fragility of our world.

But knowing as communion underscores that the goal of our ventures is not an endpoint, a conclusion from which we turn and walk away. It is the onset of a dynamic, healthy, relationship. Where insight leads to the sense of future prospects, insight inaugurates deepening insight. Communion underscores that knowing is stewardly care. It underscores that knowing is born of love; communion is the flowering of that love. Friendship is "the continual freshness of the other," as one philosopher calls it.

Can our knowing ventures prove damaging, despite our best intentions? Sadly, of course. But a loving-in-order-to-know approach at least seeks and aspires to communion, and it recognizes that communion itself sustains an ever-deepening understanding and mutuality of knower and known.

Beauty

It is difficult to put words on beauty; thankfully, it is needless to do so. The resolution, healing, and shalom that love-prompted knowing engenders may well involve beauty. Creative artistry is itself a knowing venture. And we have seen that we may indwell subsidiaries artfully. An integrative pattern, in any sort of knowing venture, that artfully melds particulars and betokens even richer reality may well be beautiful. The beautiful products of such integrations bring beauty to other people and places and things. As one writer says, beauty says, "All will be well." Beauty promises and evokes shalom.

Joy

Where knowing begins from love and involves healthful, ongoing, unfolding, relatedness to the real, there is epistemic value to delight, and there is cause for joy throughout. Love and wonder which prompt a notice and then a regard that invites the real involves a grateful, humble sense of the "might not be." This sense persists and even escalates with the peace of resolution and ongoing communion.

We have let joy become, in many circumstances of life, curiously alien. But joy in our work and in our knowing ventures always signposts a truer, hospitable world in which we are at home, a world that is among us, growingly present to the patiently grown insight of love.

Everyday adventures in knowing for shalom

Our knowing ventures—from everyday ones to grand, lifelong ones—aspire to shalom. Every venture longs for it; every insight brings shalom, if only in the tiniest measure.

Students entering college long for the resolution of completed education, fully developed humanness, fulfilled dreams, acquired expertise, peaceable and productive contribution to the world. Business and design teams seek to develop effective products and service, for value, for the good of communities, for long-term sustainability. Their products may, in fact, bring shalom. Artists seek beauty and reality and truth. Their audiences are the recipients of shalom. Doctors and counselors and gardeners seek flourishing, resulting in restored health and life. People serving others seek and implement proposals to the end of shalom. To seek healthy relationship of any sort is to seek peace in that relationship. Even a lowly search for car keys is a knowing venture that seeks and restores shalom. No knowing venture is too small to be about shalom.

Power or peace?

Knowing ventures, on the loving-to-know approach, culminate in communion and shalom. The loving-to-know approach brings shalom to the knowing venture itself. Here at the end of this *Little Manual*, the vision of shalom offers a final point of contrast and choice. Once we understand the options for knowing, we have a choice to make about our orientation, our posture. We can choose knowledge as information, indifferently, impersonally, passively amassed, to the end of a comprehensive package. Or we can choose the posture of loving in order to know, and knowing to the end of communion.

Putting the two alongside each other shows up the knowledge-as-information epistemology as an implicit disrespect. It depersonalizes the yet-to-be-known. It fails to confer dignity, to accord space, to offer welcome. It dictates the terms, the way we want our knowledge to come to us. It is uncaring about reality.

The knowledge-as-information approach is about power. It lives up to Francis Bacon's sixteenth-century summons to modernity: Knowledge is power. The point of knowledge is to eliminate wonder and mystery. It's to put humans in control of the world.

Knowledge as information lends itself to commodification. Knowledge is quantifiable, usable to bring wealth and mastery. This approach obviously targets and reaps results. But results and shalom are two different things. Results, over time, can lead to damage, even as power corrupts. We live in a results-driven society. To work with the society you do have to be about results, it seems.

Epistemic posture and our humanness

But if the loving-in-order-to-know vision is true, it also rings true to human persons. It rings true at a deeper level, a level closer to who we really are. Deep down every one of us cares and loves, and longs for care and love. The knowledge-as-information approach has sidelined care and love; it has sidelined who we are. Knowledge, it tells us, is not about these things. It's about information. And if it's about anything else, it's about progress and power. Feelings are private and only impede the important job of knowledge. Epistemological dualism like this dehumanizes. Its practice invites unhealth.

The knowledge-as-information approach excludes the loving-in-order-to-know approach. But loving in order to know is an orientation that we can tap everywhere, even in alien situations. And when we do, it makes us better at our knowing ventures, and it brings shalom.

Better information and results

Rejecting the knowledge-as-information epistemology actually makes us better at knowledge-as-information. Bringing love and responsible care to our knowing venture is giving ourselves—our whole selves—to it. To live in love deepens us as persons and knowers. It yields better knowers and knowing. It frees us to the courage and play of imagination and innovation. This invites the real more respectfully, and so it yields better results and better quality, results that are truer to reality. It yields better information.

It may not lead to immediate wealth or domination. Over the long run, however, it yields healthier fruit. It yields, not the power of domination, but the more fruitful bond of friendship. It should bring shalom. It's the difference between a domination that is actually false to life, and a stewardship that rings true. Knowing is like tending the fruit trees of reality. Investing care in the tending makes for a happier tree and yields better fruit. Loving in order to know brings to reality the personal care that invites its healing and wholeness. And that reaps dividends. Loving to know is actually a smarter investment strategy.

In fact, the knowledge-as-information approach actually self-destructs, even as it destroys us and the world. SFI shows up the contradictions at the heart of the knowledge-as-information approach. If knowledge is information, how do you come to know in the first place? Either you have knowledge or you don't. If you don't have it, you don't get it. If knowledge is clear information, how can there be such a thing as coming to understand? How can everything be clear all at once? How can it all be focal? And in any case, focusing on information is the very thing that blinds us to its meaning. It involves the very distrust that prevents the humility and self-giving it takes to move forward to insight.

So where we think we have been successful on a knowledge-as-information approach we should see whether we were in fact importing features of SFI without realizing it. How much better we will be at knowing as we notice these features and cultivate them intentionally?

The choice between the two approaches to knowing, then, is a choice about effectiveness. But it is a choice about effectiveness because it is first a choice about who we are, and who we want to be, as human persons and as knowers. We must ask: What do we think lies at the core of who we are, and in our moments of deepest, truest being? Power and domination prove to be a false and damaging objective. Love, even when our lives are fraught with challenges to it, rings true again and again. Might it not be truer to live true to who we are?

Being true to the vision of shalom

Our choice is also a choice about how we want to see life. Is a vision of life, of reality, as finally about love and shalom something that we can believe? Or are we compelled to think that ultimately reality is personless, meaningless, chaotic, warring? The latter is well-suited to seeking power and domination. For if that is all there is, it doesn't matter how we treat it. In the face of meaninglessness, domination is a better strategy.

But the vision of shalom cannot be false, if it is to be itself. We have to really think this in order to seek it. Is it wishful thinking? Yes, definitely. But it is not delusional. It is true—not in the sense of correct, certain information. It is true in the sense of troth. Troth is the old word for a pledge or covenant. We pledge to this vision of life. It is true in the sense of a T-square or a plumbline. This vision brings reality in line with itself. In this we recognize knowing's necessary dimension of covenant. We choose to *be* . . . true.

The "end" of the venture

Here we are at the end of this *Little Manual*. Quite possibly your knowing venture is nearing its end also. It's worth thinking about the mystery of this end.

To move, in love and pledge, through invitation and indwelling, to undergo encounter and transformation, cultivating dance and communion to the end of shalom, is not exactly to arrive with exhaustive finality at what we sought, and not exactly to be finished with the adventure.

In fact, at the outset, we set out to pursue an end we did not yet know, or only half-understood. That we could actually do this is a telltale mark of the adventure that is human knowing. We struggled to relate to apparent clues in a different way, prompting a fresh integrative pattern. Then, as we have been graced to know and be known in the encounter of insight, we find ourselves transformed, embedded more deeply in a changed reality, one that is fraught with meaning and pregnant with future prospects. We are in a new world. What we have sought and found proves to be different from and richer than what we thought it was going to be. But far from this being a matter of alienation we find ourselves more profoundly at home.

Nor are we finished with the adventure. For the end of the venture is ongoing relational communion of knower and known. The only way that this would end would be for us to walk away from the relationship. In the context of this covenantal approach to knowing, walking away would be something like "the secretary will disavow any knowledge of your existence"—a line familiar to any watcher of the *Mission: Impossible* television and film series—a line that disconcertingly signals abrogation of covenant. No, where possible, we move forward in relationship and peace. Additionally, our venture and its end expand our felt, subsidiary grasp of things as we pursue its, and other, prospects.

Our knowing ventures are graced to reach their end. But this is "end" in the sense of fulfillment and resolution. It often proves to be another beginning. The college experience underscores this in one graphic word: commencement.

The idea of commencement additionally suggests what we adventurers, on attaining this end, should do. It calls for celebration—a festive ceremony. Indeed, where we love in order to know, we might treat this as a kind of anniversary.

Here at the end of your knowing venture, celebrate the pilgrimage and celebrate the gift. And go on your way rejoicing.

Exercises for your knowing venture

1. Compare and contrast the knowledge-as-information epistemic approach with the loving-in-order-to-know epistemic approach. What are for you the most significant differences?

2. Review the positive effects that a loving-in-order-to-know approach has had on your knowing venture. What negative impact has it had?

3. Do you agree that we live in a culture that is committed to the knowledge-as-information approach? Discuss the impact of this on knowing ventures, on knowers, and on reality.

4. What does it look like to live out a loving-in-order-to-know approach in such a culture? Suggest ways that you can influence and reshape the prevailing cultural outlook on knowing.

5. Describe some things that pertain when shalom reigns. Is the vision of shalom true?

6. Describe some ways that your knowing venture has been, or is, knowing for shalom.

7. Describe some knowing ventures that have not brought shalom. What would be ways your venture might not be knowing for shalom?

8. How has joy attended your knowing venture? Do you agree that joy signposts shalom? Discuss this.

9. Reflect together over the journey of your knowing venture. Devise a plan to celebrate your "commencement."

Some Notes on Sources

WITH ONE NOTABLE EXCEPTION, all the authors and works that shape this *Little Manual* are properly referenced and expounded upon in *Loving to Know: Introducing Covenant Epistemology* (Cascade, 2011), (L2K). But here I want briefly to credit the sources of some of the themes in this *Little Manual*.

Love

Part 1's title, "pilgrimage," reflects missiologist Lesslie Newbigin's idea of being on the way to knowing: *Proper Confidence: Faith, Doubt and Certainty in Christian Discipleship* (Grand Rapids: Eerdmans, 1995).

In chapter 1, as well as reflected in the title of Part 2, the notion of reality as gift is drawn from theologian Phillip Rolnick's *Person, Grace, and God* (Grand Rapids: Eerdmans, 2007). The idea of reality as personal comes from many places, but certainly from Parker Palmer's work: *To Know as We are Known: Education as a Spiritual Journey* (San Francisco: HarperSanFrancisco, 1966), and *The Courage to Teach: Exploring the Inner Landscape of a Teacher's Life* (San Francisco: Jossey-Bass, 1998).

"Let there be" is language from the beginning chapter of Genesis, the first book in the Holy Bible. Covenant epistemology draws the idea of covenant as relationship from Michael Williams' *Far as the Curse is Found: The Covenant Story of Redemption.* (Phillipsburg, NJ: Presbyterian & Reformed, 2005).

Colin Gunton, in *The One, the Three and the Many* (Cambridge: Cambridge University Press, 1993), avers that love is at the core of all things. Active receptivity is a theme in the work of Simone Weil, *Waiting for God*, translated by Emma Craufurd, (New York: HarperCollins, 2001). It is Pope John Paul II who says so memorably, "Love is the gift of the self," in *Man and Woman He Created Them: A Theology of the Body*, translated by Michael Waldstein (Boston: Pauline, 2006). This is a book I have started into since the writing of L2K. The idea of consent to being reflects the thought of Jonathan Edwards as described in Roland Delattre's "Jonathan Edwards and the Recovery of Aesthetics for Religious Ethics" (*Journal of Religious Ethics* 31.2 [2003] 277–97).

David Bentley Hart's, *The Beauty of the Infinite: The Aesthetics of Christian Truth* (Grand Rapids: Eerdmans, 2003) is the one notable exception to which I referred above. I have gotten more deeply into this work in the last year. And while L2K accords Hart a mention, this *Little Manual* displays his work's widening influence on covenant epistemology, specifically here his conviction that shalom, not violence, is the ultimate reality.

Pledge

This chapter is shaped by a deep working understanding of Michael Polanyi's epistemology. Find a reference to his some of his works below (see "Indwelling"). Specifically, Polanyi is the origin of the understanding of commitment as a manner of disposing ourselves toward the world, toward what we do not yet know. Parker Palmer is the educator credited with developing the idea of truth as troth (see "Love," above).

Invitation

Personhood as being-in-communion comes from the work of John Macmurray. *Persons in Relation* (Atlantic Highlands, NJ: Humanities Press International, 1991). Dan Allender is the therapist and author of *The Healing Path: How the Hurts in Your Past Can Lead You to a More Abundant Life* (Colorado Springs, CO: Waterbrook, 2000). The important account of the four dimensions of humanness comes from James Loder's work, *The Transforming Moment*, 2nd ed. (Colorado Springs, CO: Helmers and Howard, 1989). His account of the knowing event is schematized in figure 3. And covenant epistemology's theme of the face, or gaze, of the loving other is drawn in part from his work.

Although the theme draws from several sources, the phrase, felt body sense, originates distinctively from psychotherapist Eugene Gendlin's *Focusing* (New York: Bantam, 1979). The idea of welcome is inspired by George Steiner's *Real Presences* (Chicago: University of Chicago Press, 1989). Henri Nouwen originates the wonderful definition of hospitality as creating a warm and welcoming space: *Reaching Out: The Three Movements of the Spiritual Life* (New York: Doubleday, 1975).

Indwelling

The *Little Manual* owes a great debt to philosopher-turned-scientist Michael Polanyi for the innovative and freeing epistemology he developed. Subsidiary-focal integration, indwelling, and temporary analysis, are his invention. These motifs permeate his work but are especially accessible in some of the essays in *Knowing and Being: Essays by Michael Polanyi*, edited by Marjorie Grene, University of Chicago Press, 1969), and in "Tacit Knowing," in *The Tacit Dimension*, foreword by Amartya Sen, (Chicago: University of Chicago Press, 2009). The three dimensions of clues, the normative, our felt body sense, and the situation, reflect theologian John Frame's triad in *The Doctrine of the Knowledge of God* (Phillipsburg, NJ: Presbyterian & Reformed, 1987).

Encounter

"Contact with reality" is also Polanyi's phrase, along with the idea of indeterminate future manifestations. I took the former as the title of my PhD dissertation; my next writing project I hope will be a revision of that work as *Contact with Reality: Polanyi's Realism and its Value for Christian Faith*. Martin Buber originates the notion of I-You encounter, in his book, *I and Thou*, translated by Walter Kaufmann, (New York: Scribner's, 1970).

Transformation

The *Little Manual* draws the phrases "transformation" and "the knowing event" from James Loder (see "Invitation," above).

Dance

The motif of dance comes from theologian Colin Gunton's recent forwarding of the fourth-century Cappadocian church fathers' proposal of *perichoresis* to express the particularity and relatedness of the Holy Trinity (see "Love" above). This chapter reflects again Hart's understanding of reality as ultimately shalom (also see "Love" above).

Shalom

Again, Hart's influence is evident. The definition of friendship, as the continual freshness of the other, is Phil Rolnick's (see "Love," above). That beauty says, "all will be well," comes from John and Staci Eldredge, *Captivating: Unveiling the Mystery of a Woman's Soul* (Nashville: Thomas Nelson, 2005).